Editor
Tracy Edmunds

Managing Editor
Ina Massler Levin, M.A.

Editor-in-Chief
Sharon Coan, M.S. Ed.

Cover Artist
Tony Carrillo

Art Manager
Kevin Barnes

Art Director
CJae Froshay

Imaging
Rosa C. See

Product Manager
Phil Garcia

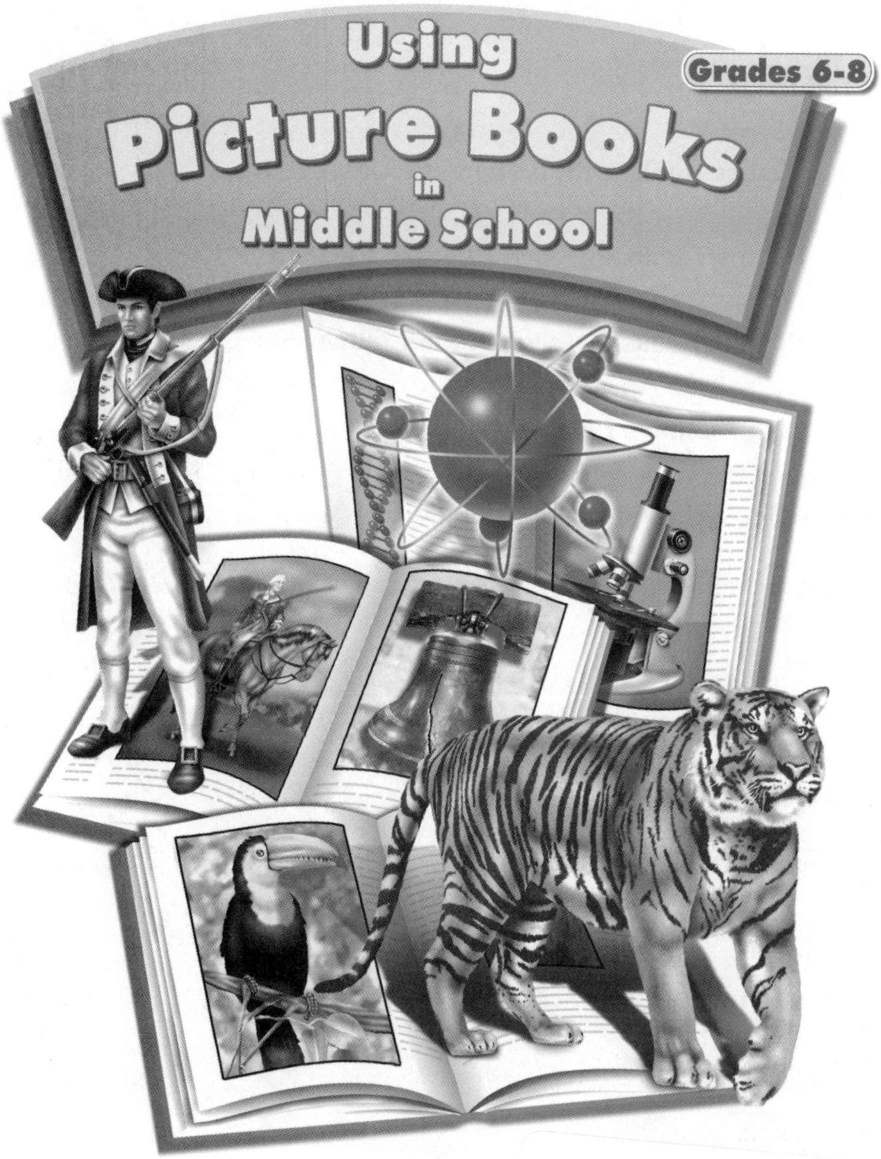
Using
Picture Books
in
Middle School
Grades 6-8

Dr. Allyson McGill
English

…ers
Rachelle Cracchiolo, M.S. Ed.
Mary Dupuy Smith, M.S. Ed.

Author
Kim Christi

D1411354

Teacher Created Materials

Teacher Created Materials, Inc.
6421 Industry Way
Westminster, CA 92683
www.teachercreated.com
ISBN-0-7439-3394-X

©2004 Teacher Created Materials, Inc.
Made in U.S.A.

The classroom teacher may reproduce copies of materials in this book for classroom use only. The reproduction of any part for an entire school or school system is strictly prohibited. No part of this publication may be transmitted, stored, or recorded in any form without written permission from the publisher.

Table of Contents

Introduction

Purpose of This Book

You are teaching reading and writing to your students and trying to help them understand the main idea and supporting details of a story, and they don't get it. You are a science or history teacher trying to teach your students about how the brain works, or about the causes and effects of slavery, and they don't get it. You've gone over the material, identified the important facts, and when you look around the classroom, you see glassy stares looking back at you. You know, the looks that say, "I don't get it!" Your main objective is to help your students acquire a deep understanding of the material you need to cover. You want them to do more than just memorize facts—you want them to learn and understand. How can you take these concepts and break them down for true understanding, and present them in a way that will be more interesting for your students? Read on, and find out.

Picture Books

- Picture books provide teachers with a new and exciting way to teach.
- Picture books help teach concepts that kids just don't get.
- Picture books make learning interesting and enjoyable.

This book shows you how to choose a picture book, what to do with it after reading it to the class, and how you can apply that teaching and learning to other media, such as novels, textbooks, and Internet information. This book includes a bibliography to help you get started in your search for the right picture books to use with your students, graphic organizers that will help your students acquire a deeper understanding of the material they are reading, and plenty of examples to help you integrate picture books into your curriculum.

Picture books are for everyone, and as you work your way through this book you will begin to see how they can be used to teach a variety of concepts across the curriculum. You will find out quickly how much your students love picture books. They will look forward to that read aloud time when they have the opportunity to explore a new picture book. There are so many great picture books available for all ages that you will have no trouble finding a selection your students will love.

Introduction *(cont.)*

Graphic Organizers

- After reading a picture book, graphic organizers can be used to help teach concepts from the book.

- Difficult concepts can be taught in a visual format using graphic organizers.

- Graphic organizers can be used across the curriculum.

- Graphic organizers can be used with picture books, literature circles, textbooks, or any other form of media.

- Graphic organizers provide you with a visual assessment of student understanding.

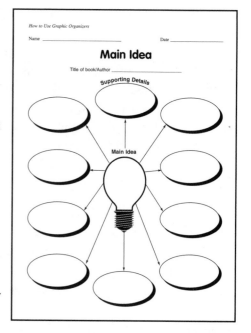

Once you see how to use picture books and graphic organizers together to teach the concepts included in this book, you will discover how much fun it is to use picture books to teach, and students will discover how much fun it is to learn with picture books. Remember, you don't have to use a graphic organizer every time you use a picture book. You can alternate between group discussions for understanding, personal reflections, and graphic organizers to assist students in reading for understanding.

How to Use This Book

How do you get started? All you have to do is decide what you are going to teach and then find the picture books that will help you teach that lesson. Let's take this one step at a time and walk through planning a lesson together.

- First, decide what concept you want to teach your students.

- Choose your picture book. Browse through the list of picture books beginning on page 74 for ideas on what type of picture book might work best for your lesson. Your school or local library is a great place to find picture books. Take a few minutes to read suitable picture books and choose the one that best fits your needs.

- Decide if you will use a graphic organizer. This book contains a variety of graphic organizers that can be used with any lesson you teach. Detailed examples showing how to use these tools are provided with each set of organizers. Be sure to fill out a copy of the graphic organizer for yourself so you can guide students.

- Read the picture book aloud to the class.

- Discuss the book and/or complete the graphic organizer with your students.

Using Picture Books with a Thematic Unit

No matter what subject you teach, using picture books in conjunction with a thematic unit will enhance the learning environment in your classroom. The section of this book titled *Designing Your Thematic Unit Using Picture Books* is an example of how to integrate picture books and graphic organizers to teach a variety of concepts within a thematic unit. Once you have experienced the use of picture books to teach concepts, you will be able to create the thematic units you need to integrate with your curriculum.

Using Picture Books to Teach Literary Elements

This section of the book provides you with many different examples of how to teach literary elements through the use of picture books and graphic organizers. Though the examples here use only one book, literary elements can be taught using a wide variety of picture books. A short list of picture books for teaching literary elements can be found in the bibliography (p. 74) and you will find many more at your library.

Once students understand the literary concepts you are teaching using the picture books, move on to the more difficult media of novels. Whether your literature circles consist of multiple novels or a whole class of novels, the literary concepts taught through the use of picture books can transfer over to novels very easily. In fact, you can continue to use graphic organizers with novels as a way to check for student understanding. These graphic organizers will provide you with information on whether students understand literary concepts, and will also enable you to check on comprehension as students read a variety of literature in your class.

Using Picture Books in the Content Areas

Picture books can be used to teach science, social studies, and even math. Multiple picture books can be used to teach content in one area, or one picture book can be used to teach concepts from many different disciplines. You can also use several different graphic organizers with one book. The graphic organizers in this book can be used over and over again with a variety of different picture books, which should allow students to develop a deeper understanding of the concept being taught.

Using Picture Books with a Thematic Unit *(cont.)*

The use of picture books in a thematic unit can bring a whole new dimension of learning to your classroom. Picture books allow your students to use an additional form of media to help them understand difficult concepts. There are a variety of picture books available and they are able to present information in a new and exciting way for students.

This section of the book will show you how to use picture books in a thematic unit, and uses the theme *Freedom in America* as an example.

To use picture books in a thematic unit:

- Clarify the important concepts you will teach to your students. In the example, an organizing web is used to identify the main ideas that will be presented in a unit about freedom in America. District or state standards should also be used to identify concepts that will be taught during the unit.

- Find picture books that match each concept in the unit. There is a bibliography on page 74 that lists picture books for many different themes. Librarians can also be very helpful in identifying appropriate picture books. Read through as many picture books as possible and identify the ones that are best suited to your theme concepts.

- Decide which graphic organizers you will use with which book. For each picture book, choose a graphic organizer that fits the concept being taught. For example, the first picture book read in the Freedom in America unit is *Coming to America, The Story of Immigration*. This book provides a historical overview of immigration in America. A sequencing organizer is used so students can create a timeline, giving them a historical reference for the entire unit.

- Create a sequence for presenting the picture books and graphic organizers during the unit. The Freedom in America unit presents books in a historical timeline, beginning with the arrival of the pilgrims and moving on through the importation of African slaves, the arrival of Ellis Island immigrants, and the rise of the civil rights movement. At the end of the unit, fictional stories are used to discuss the concept of war.

Designing a Thematic Unit Using Picture Books

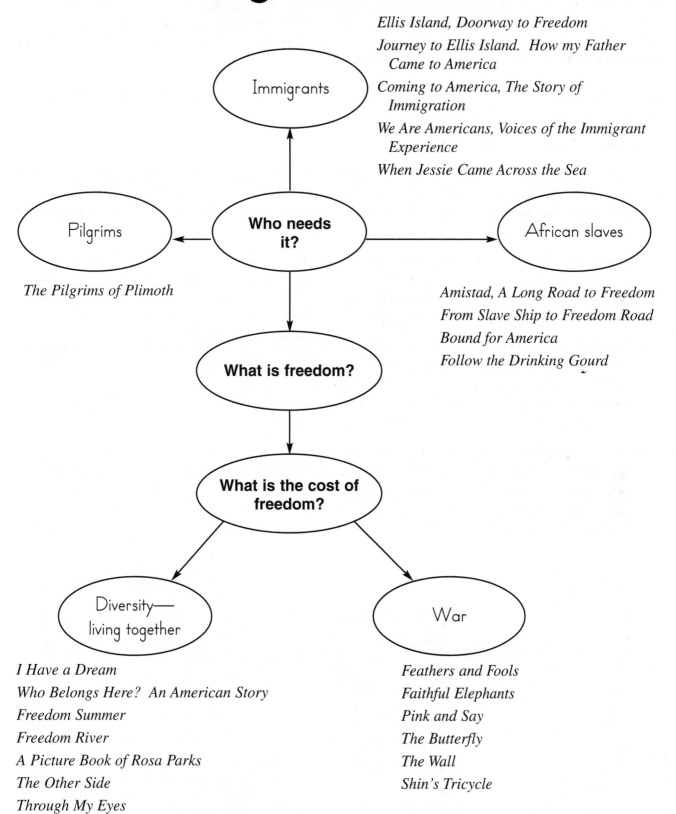

Ellis Island, Doorway to Freedom

Journey to Ellis Island. How my Father Came to America

Coming to America, The Story of Immigration

We Are Americans, Voices of the Immigrant Experience

When Jessie Came Across the Sea

Immigrants

Pilgrims

Who needs it?

African slaves

The Pilgrims of Plimoth

Amistad, A Long Road to Freedom
From Slave Ship to Freedom Road
Bound for America
Follow the Drinking Gourd

What is freedom?

What is the cost of freedom?

Diversity— living together

War

I Have a Dream
Who Belongs Here? An American Story
Freedom Summer
Freedom River
A Picture Book of Rosa Parks
The Other Side
Through My Eyes

Feathers and Fools
Faithful Elephants
Pink and Say
The Butterfly
The Wall
Shin's Tricycle

Sequencing

The following is from *Coming to America, The Story of Immigration* by Betsy Maestro (Scholastic, 1996). This example creates a timeline to help students understand the history involved in this unit.

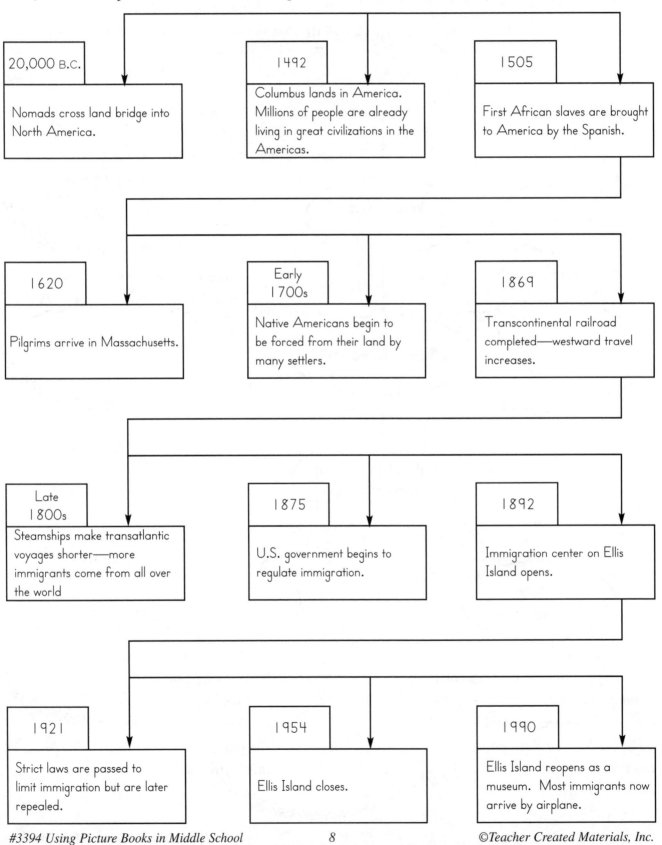

20,000 B.C. Nomads cross land bridge into North America.	**1492** Columbus lands in America. Millions of people are already living in great civilizations in the Americas.	**1505** First African slaves are brought to America by the Spanish.
1620 Pilgrims arrive in Massachusetts.	**Early 1700s** Native Americans begin to be forced from their land by many settlers.	**1869** Transcontinental railroad completed—westward travel increases.
Late 1800s Steamships make transatlantic voyages shorter—more immigrants come from all over the world	**1875** U.S. government begins to regulate immigration.	**1892** Immigration center on Ellis Island opens.
1921 Strict laws are passed to limit immigration but are later repealed.	**1954** Ellis Island closes.	**1990** Ellis Island reopens as a museum. Most immigrants now arrive by airplane.

Main Idea and Supporting Details

The following is from *The Pilgrims of Plimoth* by Marcia Sewall (Scholastic, 1986). This example identifies just one reason people came to America, religious freedom.

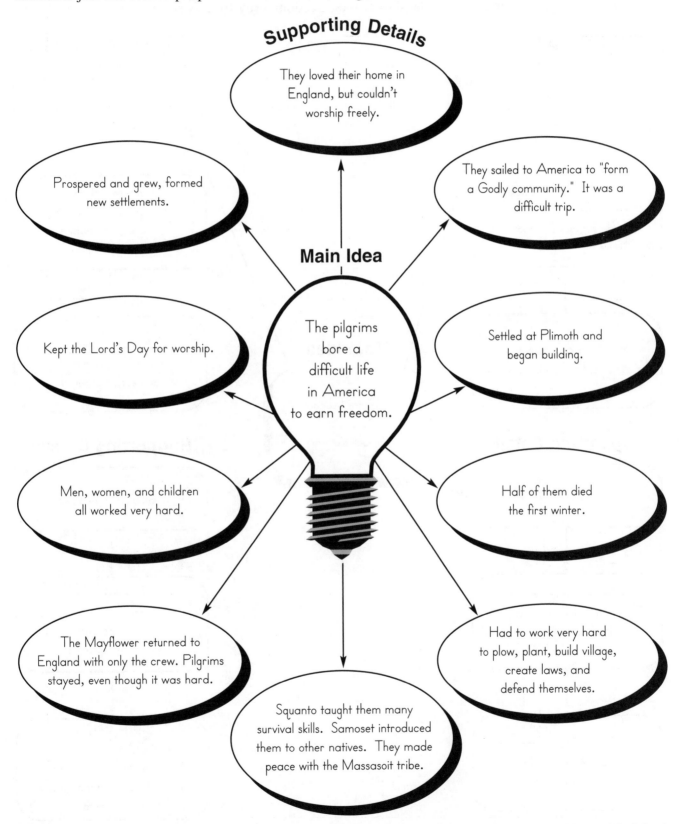

Supporting Details

They loved their home in England, but couldn't worship freely.

They sailed to America to "form a Godly community." It was a difficult trip.

Prospered and grew, formed new settlements.

Main Idea

Settled at Plimoth and began building.

Kept the Lord's Day for worship.

The pilgrims bore a difficult life in America to earn freedom.

Men, women, and children all worked very hard.

Half of them died the first winter.

The Mayflower returned to England with only the crew. Pilgrims stayed, even though it was hard.

Had to work very hard to plow, plant, build village, create laws, and defend themselves.

Squanto taught them many survival skills. Samoset introduced them to other natives. They made peace with the Massasoit tribe.

Main Idea and Supporting Details

This example is taken from the books *From Slave Ship to Freedom Road* by Julius Lester (Dial, 1998) and *Bound for America* by James Haskins & Kathleen Benson (Lothrop, Lee, 1999). This example can be used to help students understand how slavery took freedom away from African slaves.

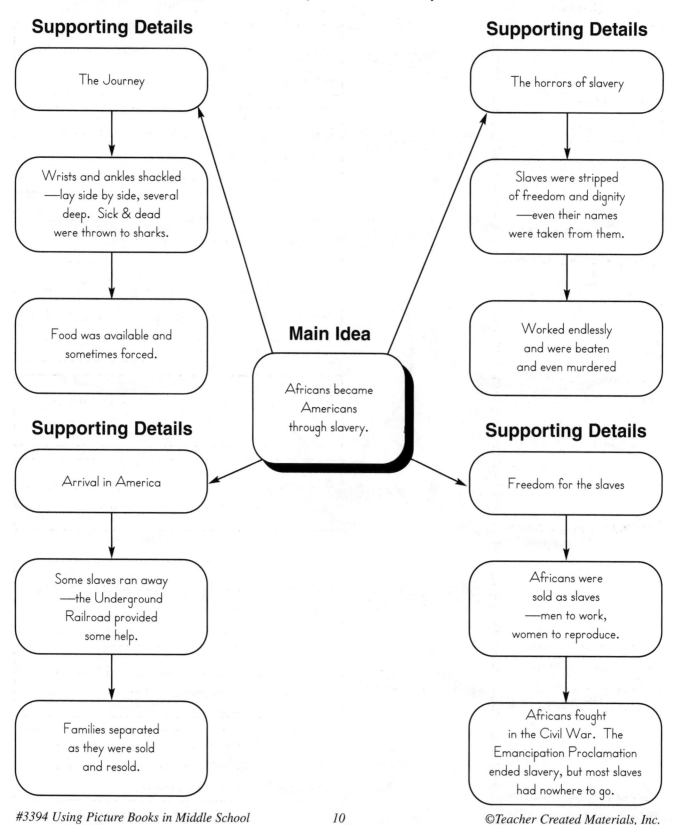

Supporting Details

The Journey

Wrists and ankles shackled —lay side by side, several deep. Sick & dead were thrown to sharks.

Food was available and sometimes forced.

Supporting Details

The horrors of slavery

Slaves were stripped of freedom and dignity —even their names were taken from them.

Worked endlessly and were beaten and even murdered

Main Idea

Africans became Americans through slavery.

Supporting Details

Arrival in America

Some slaves ran away —the Underground Railroad provided some help.

Families separated as they were sold and resold.

Supporting Details

Freedom for the slaves

Africans were sold as slaves —men to work, women to reproduce.

Africans fought in the Civil War. The Emancipation Proclamation ended slavery, but most slaves had nowhere to go.

Cause and Effect

This example is from *Ellis Island Doorway to Freedom* by Steven Kroll (Holiday, 1995) and can be used to help students understand the impact of immigration on American freedom.

Cause   **Effect**

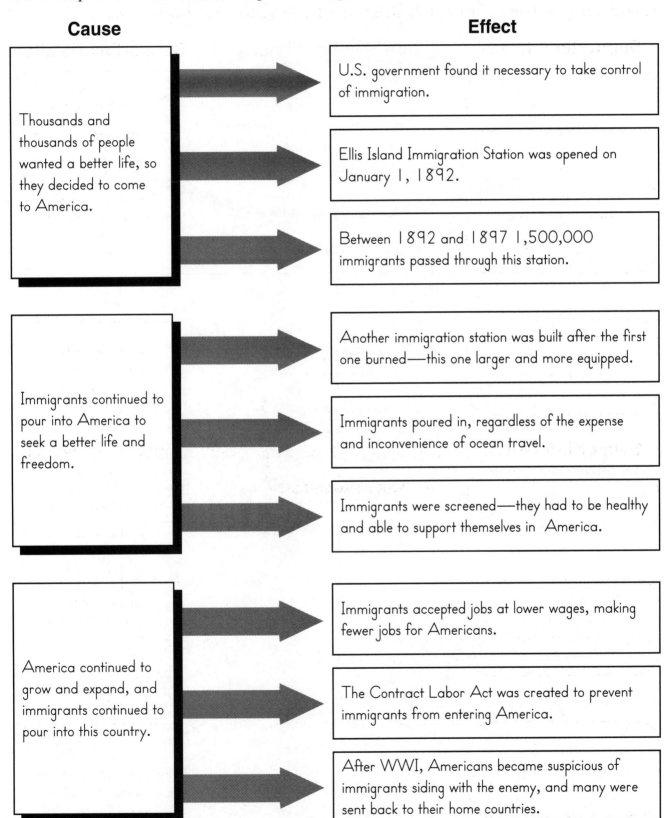

Thousands and thousands of people wanted a better life, so they decided to come to America.

→ U.S. government found it necessary to take control of immigration.

→ Ellis Island Immigration Station was opened on January 1, 1892.

→ Between 1892 and 1897 1,500,000 immigrants passed through this station.

Immigrants continued to pour into America to seek a better life and freedom.

→ Another immigration station was built after the first one burned—this one larger and more equipped.

→ Immigrants poured in, regardless of the expense and inconvenience of ocean travel.

→ Immigrants were screened—they had to be healthy and able to support themselves in America.

America continued to grow and expand, and immigrants continued to pour into this country.

→ Immigrants accepted jobs at lower wages, making fewer jobs for Americans.

→ The Contract Labor Act was created to prevent immigrants from entering America.

→ After WWI, Americans became suspicious of immigrants siding with the enemy, and many were sent back to their home countries.

Mood, Feelings, Attitude

This example is from *Who Belongs Here?: An American Story* by Margy Burns Knight (Tilbury House, 1993). This story can be used to help students understand the many emotions immigrants encounter in their search for freedom.

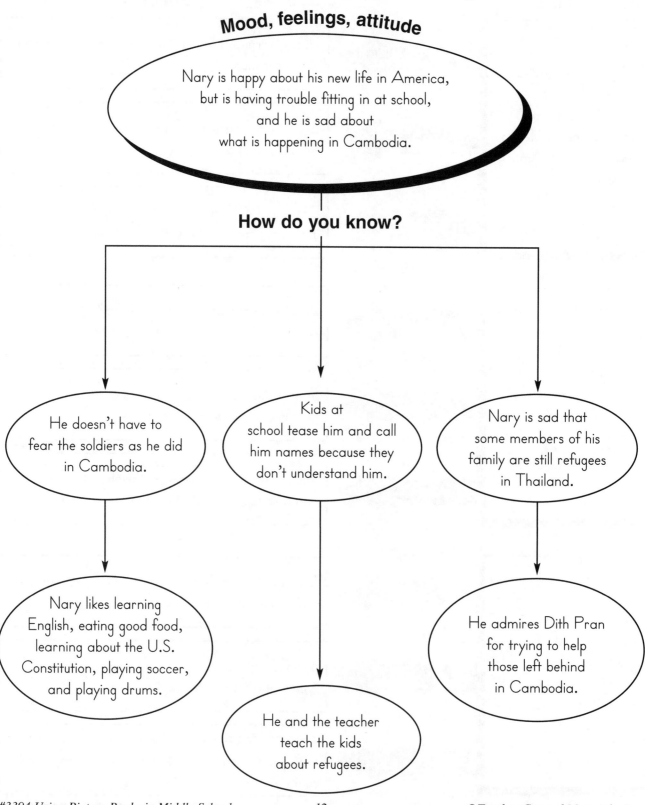

Mood, feelings, attitude

Nary is happy about his new life in America,
but is having trouble fitting in at school,
and he is sad about
what is happening in Cambodia.

How do you know?

He doesn't have to fear the soldiers as he did in Cambodia.

Kids at school tease him and call him names because they don't understand him.

Nary is sad that some members of his family are still refugees in Thailand.

Nary likes learning English, eating good food, learning about the U.S. Constitution, playing soccer, and playing drums.

He and the teacher teach the kids about refugees.

He admires Dith Pran for trying to help those left behind in Cambodia.

12

Vocabulary

This example of vocabulary was taken from *I Have a Dream* by Dr. Martin Luther King, Jr. (Scholastic, 1997)

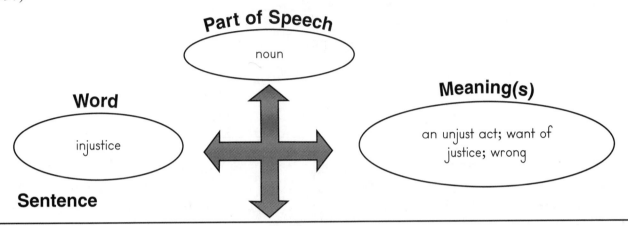

Sentence

Slavery was an act of injustice done to the African–American people.

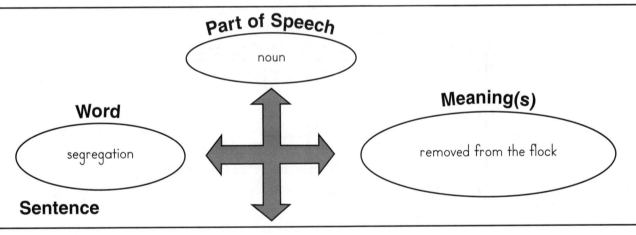

Sentence

Segregation was forced on African–American people as a way to separate them from the other Americans.

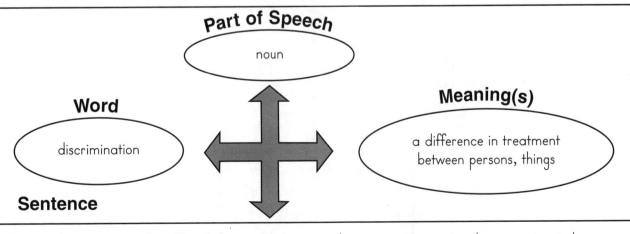

Sentence

African–American people suffered discrimination since there were many ways they were treated differently than other Americans.

Predictions

The following example is from *Feathers and Fools* by Mem Fox (Harcourt, Inc., 1989). This can be used as an introduction to war.

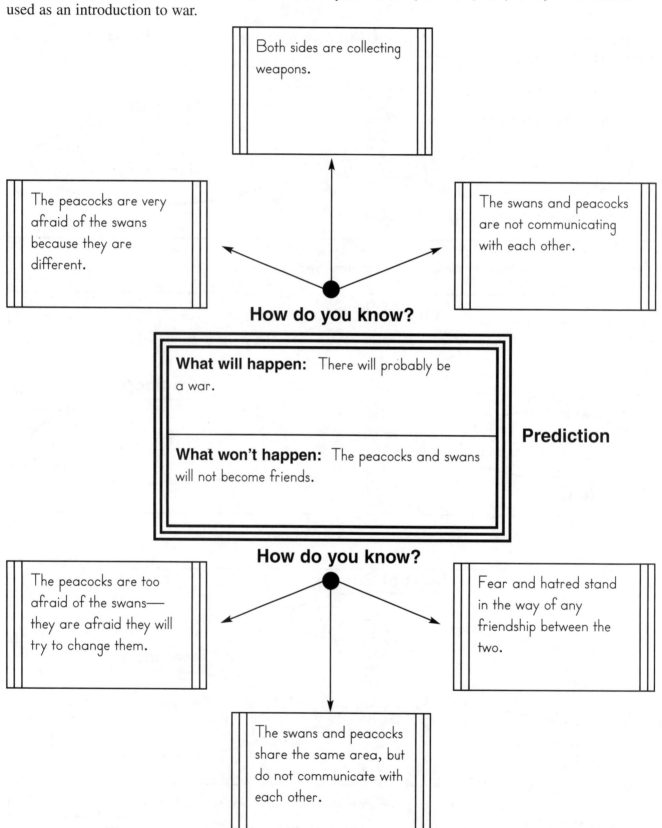

Both sides are collecting weapons.

The peacocks are very afraid of the swans because they are different.

The swans and peacocks are not communicating with each other.

How do you know?

What will happen: There will probably be a war.

What won't happen: The peacocks and swans will not become friends.

Prediction

How do you know?

The peacocks are too afraid of the swans— they are afraid they will try to change them.

Fear and hatred stand in the way of any friendship between the two.

The swans and peacocks share the same area, but do not communicate with each other.

Using Picture Books to Teach Literary Elements

Picture books are excellent for introducing students to literary concepts such as plot, setting, main idea, cause and effect, character analysis, etc.

To teach literary elements using picture books:

- Choose which concept or concepts you need to teach.

- Choose the picture book(s) that would best assist you in teaching these concepts. The picture book can match a thematic unit you are teaching, the reading level of your students, the interest of your students, or just the concept you wish to teach.

- Read the picture book(s) aloud to your class.

- Use the graphic organizers with your students to support learning.

On the following pages, graphic organizers are used with the picture book *Crickwing* by Janell Cannon to teach different literary elements. One picture book can be used to teach a variety of literary concepts, or several books can be used to teach the same concept. Once students understand the concept they can transfer that understanding to something bigger, like a chapter book, a textbook, or a novel.

The advantage to using picture books is that they are short and quick to read, allowing you to use several to teach the same concept. There are many picture books that can be used to teach any concept, and since they are all different, students will be continuously challenged to identify the information for the selected graphic organizer. These graphic organizers can be used over and over again with many picture books giving students the practice they need to fully understand the concept, and challenging them with a variety of genre and stories. This should reinforce learning and allow students to develop a deeper understanding of the concept being taught.

Setting

This example, from *Crickwing* by Janell Cannon (Harcourt, 2000), can be used to direct students' attention to the setting and the effect it has on the story.

Setting	**Effects on the story**

Setting is possibly the rain forest because it mentions "forest canopy." This may take place on the ground because the author says it's far below the forest canopy.

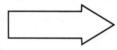

Helps the reader understand why there are strange characters in the story (leaf-cutter ants, a cockroach, an ocelot, army ants, etc.).

The rain forest is real. However, talking cockroaches and ants are not.

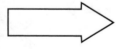

Gives the reader a clue that there might be fact as well as fiction in the story.

There are many plants and animals in the rainforest.

Crickwing has a lot of things to sculpt with and eat and animals to interact with.

Main Idea and Supporting Details

This example, from *Crickwing* by Janell Cannon (Harcourt, 2000), assists students in identifying the main idea and supporting details.

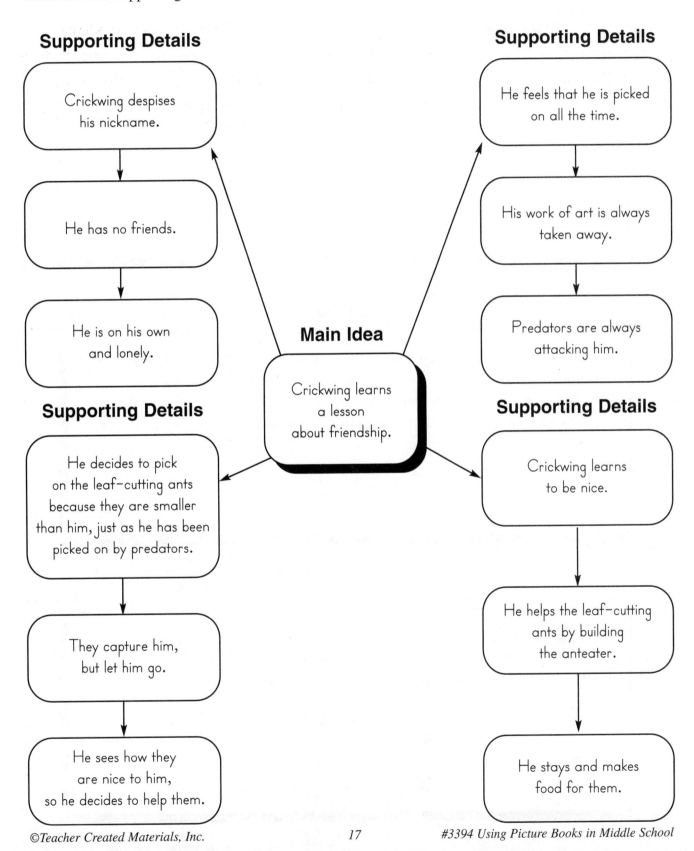

Supporting Details

Crickwing despises his nickname.

He has no friends.

He is on his own and lonely.

Supporting Details

He feels that he is picked on all the time.

His work of art is always taken away.

Predators are always attacking him.

Main Idea

Crickwing learns a lesson about friendship.

Supporting Details

He decides to pick on the leaf-cutting ants because they are smaller than him, just as he has been picked on by predators.

They capture him, but let him go.

He sees how they are nice to him, so he decides to help them.

Supporting Details

Crickwing learns to be nice.

He helps the leaf-cutting ants by building the anteater.

He stays and makes food for them.

Sequencing

This example, from *Crickwing* by Janell Cannon (Harcourt, 2000), identifies the important pieces of a story. All three must exist to make a good story.

Beginning

Crickwing is teased because of his twisted wing. He goes off on his own to create his sculptures—only to find animals constantly picking on him and eating his "works of art" before he can finish any of them. This is beginning to make him really upset.

Middle

Crickwing gets fed-up and decides to pick on the leaf-cutting ants since they are smaller than him. The queen ant gets angry and has him captured. He is to be the peace offering for the army ants. He is taken into the forest and tied up to be left for the army ants. Two leaf-cutting ants untie him because they feel badly about leaving Crickwing for the army ants.

End

Crickwing finds out about the army ants coming to attack the leaf-cutting ants. He tells them he will save them and is taken back to their home. There he creates a sculpture of a giant anteater and scares the army ants away. He is a hero.

Fact, Fiction, or Opinions?

The following example from *Crickwing* by Janell Cannon (Harcourt, 2000) helps students understand how facts can be used in a fictional story to make it more interesting.

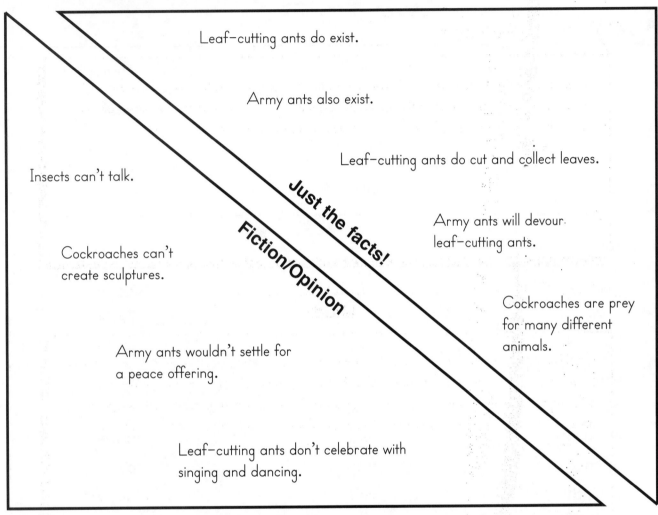

How does the author weave fact and fiction (or opinions) together to make the selection more interesting?

The author weaves together fact and fiction about cockroaches, leaf-cutting ants, and army ants to

create an entertaining story about life in the rainforest. The facts add a sense of reality, and the

fiction makes the characters interesting.

Vocabulary

This example, from *Crickwing* by Janell Cannon (Harcourt, 2000), can be used to pick out the rich vocabulary used in the story, and helps students categorize words by parts of speech.

Adjectives

shadowy	muddling	sharp-eyed
ravenous	ferocious	scaly
eensy	bright	massive
spiny	interesting	

Adverbs

clearly	carefully	never
drowsily	angrily	hard
rightfully	down	middle
below	under	toward
far	next	early
whenever	nearly	barely
often	atop	over
behind	high	drowsily

Verbs

despised	chortled	quavered
absorbed	wolfed	howled
grumbled	plummeted	gasped
cowering	snorted	yelped
darted	meddles	loomed
wailed	crowed	toil
steamed	stammered	scrambled
muttered		

Using Picture Books to Teach in the Content Areas

Because picture books use illustrations, graphics, and/or photographs in addition to text, they are perfect for teaching concepts in content areas such as science and social science.

To use picture books to teach concepts in content areas, start by looking through the bibliography on page 74 and visit your public or school library to find books that match your content and objectives. You can use picture books to introduce new concepts or review difficult ones, focus on an important historical event or person, create a timeline, or explore the causes and effects of a scientific advancement or historical event. Next, choose the graphic organizers that best fit the concept you are teaching and complete them with your students. The following graphic organizers work best with non-fiction material:

- **Main Idea and Supporting Details:** This organizer helps students pick out important information and paraphrase or summarize it. This will help students strengthen their research and expository writing skills.

- **Characteristics of . . . :** In breaking the main topic into subtopics, students have the opportunity to dig into the text for details they may otherwise skim right over. They also learn to organize facts into coherent groups.

- **Cause and Effect:** This organizer helps students identify important events and their effects.

- **Compare and Contrast:** Students find the similarities and differences between people, places, and things.

- **Fact, Fiction, or Opinion?:** This organizer is great for teaching students to differentiate between historical or scientific facts and an author's opinion, a skill that many students have difficulty with.

- **Graphic Sequencing and Timeline:** Use these organizers to create a timeline of historical events or record procedures for a scientific experiment.

- **Effects of the Setting:** Students can use this organizer to explore how the setting of a historical event affects its outcome.

- **New Vocabulary:** This organizer helps students identify, define, and apply new vocabulary in the content areas.

After using graphic organizers with picture books, you can use them to evaluate students' understanding of a concept or extend their learning. Try using graphic organizers with magazine articles, Internet articles, or even pages of your textbook.

Main Idea and Supporting Details

This example is from *Icebergs and Glaciers* written by Seymour Simon (Scholastic, 1987). Use this graphic organizer to help students pick out the important information in the book. They can then use this information to summarize or paraphrase it.

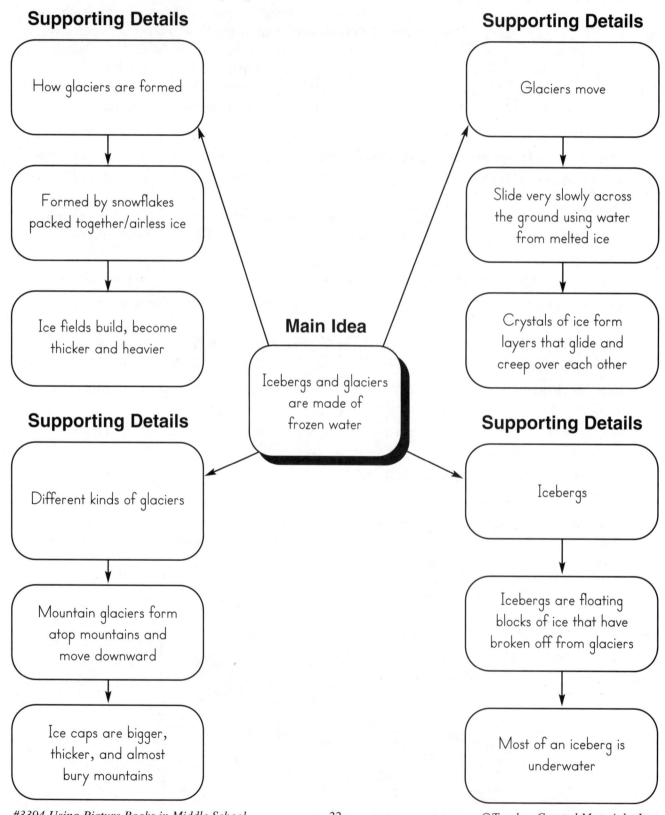

Supporting Details

How glaciers are formed

Formed by snowflakes packed together/airless ice

Ice fields build, become thicker and heavier

Supporting Details

Glaciers move

Slide very slowly across the ground using water from melted ice

Crystals of ice form layers that glide and creep over each other

Main Idea

Icebergs and glaciers are made of frozen water

Supporting Details

Different kinds of glaciers

Mountain glaciers form atop mountains and move downward

Ice caps are bigger, thicker, and almost bury mountains

Supporting Details

Icebergs

Icebergs are floating blocks of ice that have broken off from glaciers

Most of an iceberg is underwater

Characteristics of . . .

This example is also from *Icebergs and Glaciers* by Seymour Simon (Scholastic, 1987). This graphic organizer may provide students with a chance to gather more details on their topics, or it may provide them with a different way to organize them, so they can see how it fits together.

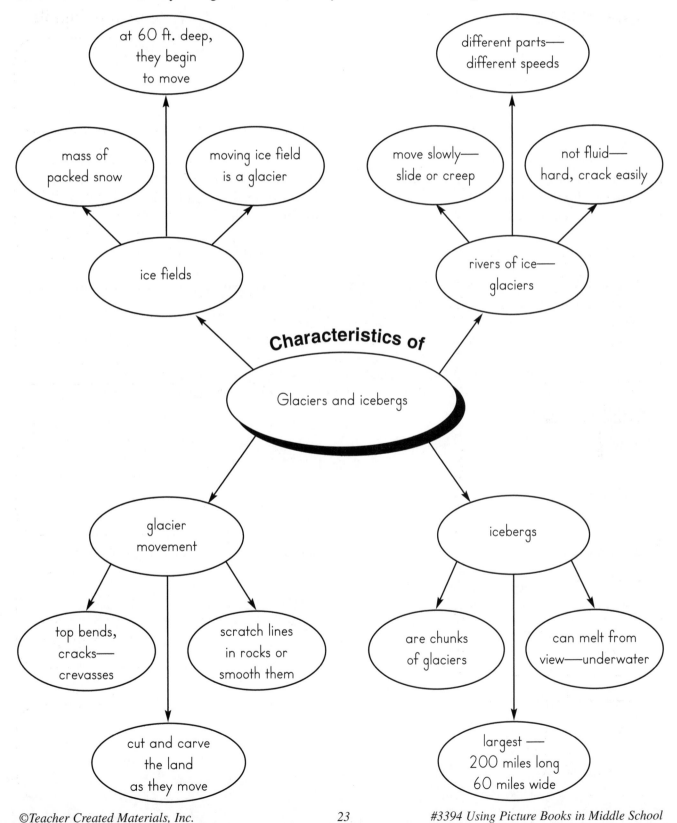

Projects to Enhance Learning

Once you have introduced a concept or several concepts to your students using picture books and graphic organizers, you can have your students apply their learning in the form of a project. Students will have fun entertaining the class with their understanding of what they have read.

Below are just a few examples of projects your students can share with the class.

- Share a picture book with a primary class.

- Turn a novel or partner book into a picture book.

- Write and illustrate a picture book using the first person ("I am the brain," "I am Ben Franklin," etc.)

- Create a brochure. Students could feature their three favorite books or a "Cast of Characters" from a book. They could each create an advertisement for the setting of a book as a place to visit, or an advertisement for the book showing the beginning, middle, and end of the story.

- Write newspaper articles covering important events or characters in a picture book.

- Create a poster persuading others to read the book, showing favorite words from the book, or detailing a character's achievements.

- Write and illustrate a timeline of the important events in the book.

- Create a multimedia presentation about a picture book. A student could show the timeline of events in a book, teach others about a character or topic, or present a commercial advertising the book.

- Write a diary from the viewpoint of the main character, a modern-day version of the story, a sequel to the story, or a "what-if" version of the story (What if Ben Franklin came back to life today?).

- Write and perform a skit showing an important event in the book.

- Create a rap or other type of song to help other students remember important concepts.

- Create a "talk show" interview of a character.

How to Use Graphic Organizers

Graphic organizers are tools that can be used in any classroom to teach any concept. After reading a picture book (or other text) you can have students complete a graphic organizer as a whole class, in small groups, or individually.

Graphic organizers are great teaching tools for many reasons:

- Graphic organizers can be used with many different forms of media. Use a graphic organizer with a picture book first to introduce a concept. Then, you can extend the learning of that concept by using the graphic organizer with a novel, textbook, video, etc.

- Students can use the graphic organizers to organize their thoughts and understand anything they read. For example, you could use the *Main Idea* organizer to help students understand the main idea and supporting details in sections of the textbook. They may find this so helpful in organizing important information that they want to use the graphic organizer throughout the book as a study tool.

- Literature circles can also benefit from the use of picture books and graphic organizers. For example, if you want students to understand the mood the author creates in the novel they are reading in their literature circle, introduce mood using a picture book and the *Mood/Feelings/Attitude* graphic organizer. Students work within their circle to identify the mood of the book and how the author creates that mood. Then, have students use the graphic organizer to identify the mood in the novel being read in their literature circle.

- Graphic organizers can help you assess student learning. For example, you can introduce a new concept through a picture book, and then watch your students fill out a graphic organizer to see if they fully understand what is being taught. This type of visual assessment allows you to check for student understanding during your instruction time. If most of your students are still having trouble understanding the concept, you can reteach the concept to the entire class using the current graphic organizer. Then, use the same graphic organizer with another picture book to teach the same concept. This will give students who already understand the concept additional practice, and students who didn't get it the first time around get additional instruction. If you still have students who don't understand after the second try, you can always pull them aside for additional one-on-one instruction.

The bibliography on page 74 of this book gives you a list of suggested picture books that can be used with each graphic organizer.

Cause and Effect

This graphic organizer can help students identify causes and effects in both fiction and non-fiction works. Cause and effect is often a difficult concept for students to understand, but one that is critical for deep learning.

To begin, choose a picture book in which causes and effects are quite evident. As students fill out the graphic organizer, you will have the opportunity to monitor understanding by glancing over their shoulders as they complete the organizer. If your students are having difficulty, complete the organizer together as a class. Then, read another picture book and allow students to try the organizer again. If your students understand the concept, move on to a picture book in which the causes and effects are more difficult to identify.

Once you are satisfied your students have acquired an appropriate understanding of this concept, you may want to reinforce their learning by using the graphic organizer with a novel, a textbook, or any other type of material.

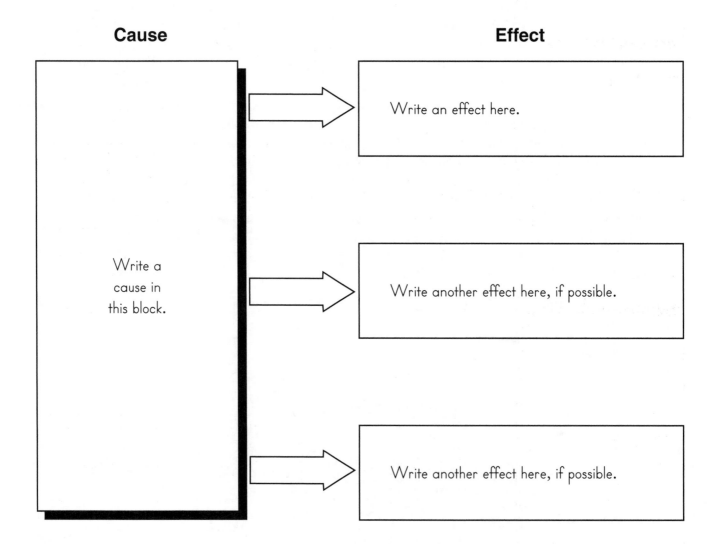

Cause

Effect

Write a cause in this block.

Write an effect here.

Write another effect here, if possible.

Write another effect here, if possible.

Cause and Effect

This example, from the picture book *Who Belongs Here? An American Story* by Margy Burns Knight (Tilbury House, 1993), introduces students to the concept of immigration.

Cause

Effect

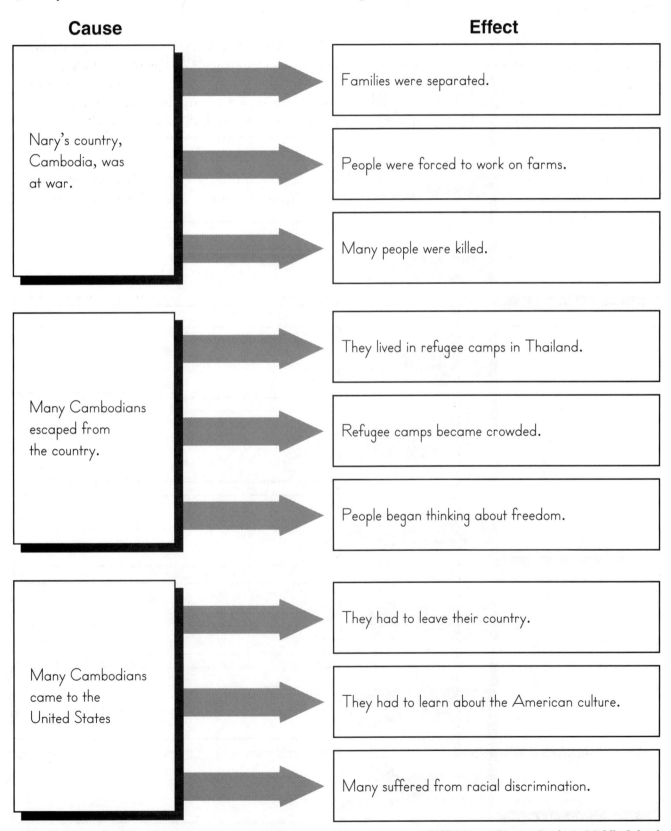

Nary's country, Cambodia, was at war.

Families were separated.

People were forced to work on farms.

Many people were killed.

Many Cambodians escaped from the country.

They lived in refugee camps in Thailand.

Refugee camps became crowded.

People began thinking about freedom.

Many Cambodians came to the United States

They had to leave their country.

They had to learn about the American culture.

Many suffered from racial discrimination.

Name _____   Date _____

Cause and Effect

_____
(title/author)

Cause   **Effect**

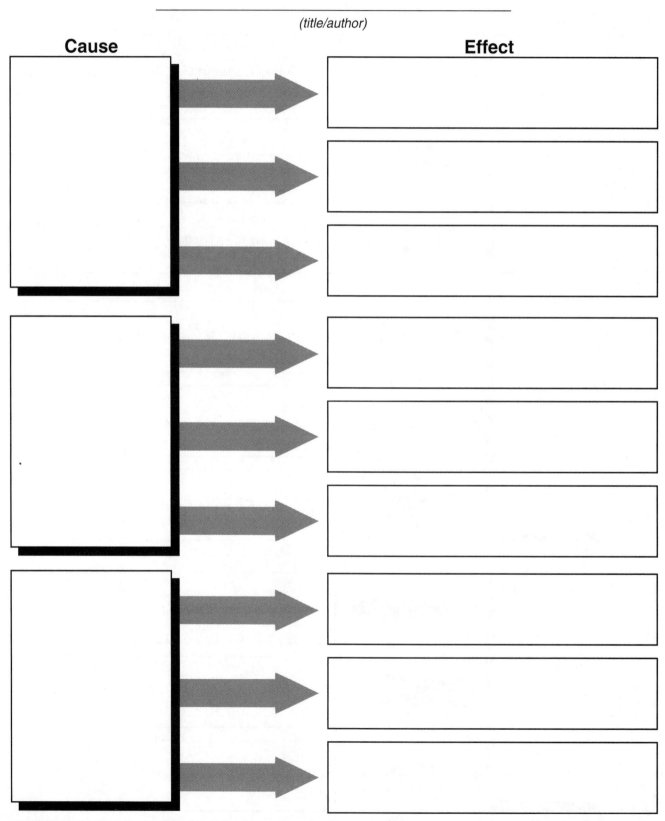

Character Analysis

The *Character Analysis* graphic organizer will help students understand the importance of "knowing the characters" in a story. Character analysis can give great insight into the root causes of events in a story, and can help students examine how an author uses character descriptions and qualities to make characters "come alive" for the reader.

The *Character Analysis* organizer can be used to describe characters using adjectives. Extend student vocabulary by calling for the use of high-quality adjectives—adjectives that are much more descriptive than "nice," "kind," or "pretty." Even if the story refers to the character as "pretty," encourage students to use the Thesaurus to find synonyms that are more descriptive.

This organizer can also be used to extend the description of characters in a piece of writing by focusing on the qualities of the characters in the story. As students read or listen they should pay attention to what the character does and how the character speaks. What accent or tone of voice might the character use? Why does the character make certain choices? Is there anything in the character's background that may explain his or her actions?

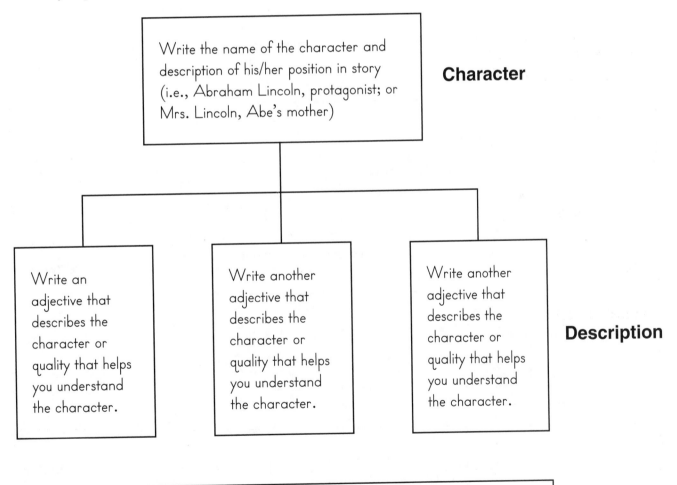

Character Analysis

This example is from *Mr. Lincoln's Way* by Patricia Polacco (Philomel Books, 2001).

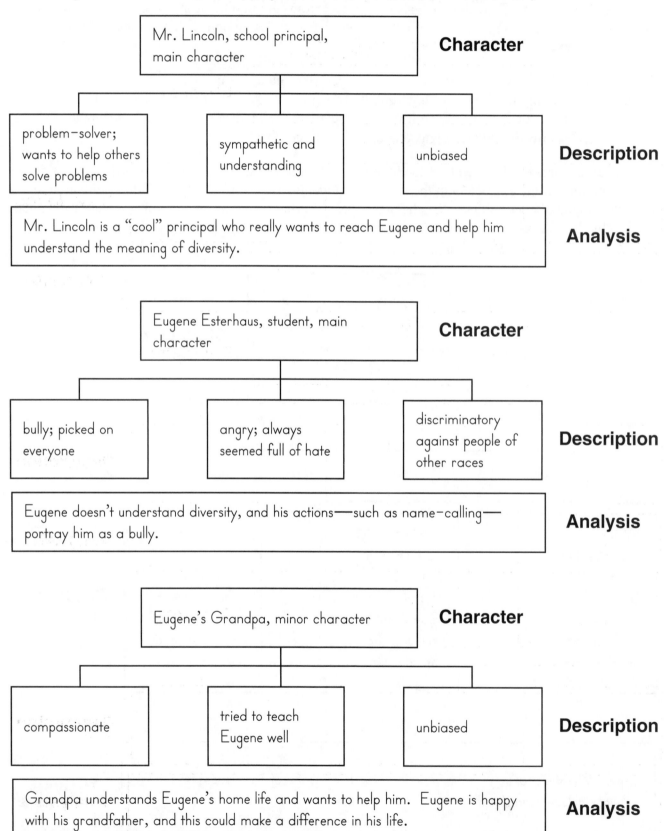

Mr. Lincoln, school principal, main character — **Character**

problem–solver; wants to help others solve problems

sympathetic and understanding

unbiased

Description

Mr. Lincoln is a "cool" principal who really wants to reach Eugene and help him understand the meaning of diversity. — **Analysis**

Eugene Esterhaus, student, main character — **Character**

bully; picked on everyone

angry; always seemed full of hate

discriminatory against people of other races

Description

Eugene doesn't understand diversity, and his actions—such as name-calling—portray him as a bully. — **Analysis**

Eugene's Grandpa, minor character — **Character**

compassionate

tried to teach Eugene well

unbiased

Description

Grandpa understands Eugene's home life and wants to help him. Eugene is happy with his grandfather, and this could make a difference in his life. — **Analysis**

Name _____   Date _____

Character Analysis

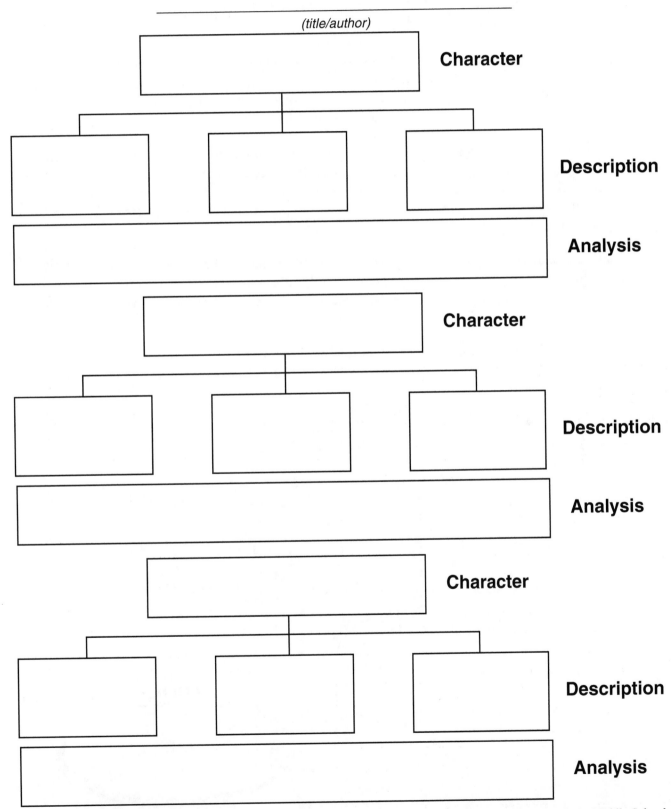

Characteristics of. . .

This generic graphic organizer leaves the concept of "characteristics" open for a variety of uses in many different subject areas. By breaking a main topic into subtopics, students have the opportunity to dig into the text for details they may otherwise skim right over.

Here are some ideas for using the *Characteristics of . . .* organizer:

In a language arts class, read a variety of picture books featuring legends, myths, and fables. Use this graphic organizer to show students the characteristics of each of these types of stories. Then, read more picture books and have students use the organizer to determine whether each is a legend, myth, or fable. You can use the same idea when teaching students about different types of poems.

In math class, read one of the math-related picture books listed in the bibliography, and use this graphic organizer to identify the characteristics of the mathematical concept featured in the story. This graphic can then be used to describe the characteristics of the math concepts students are currently learning, even if the information comes from the textbook. For example, students could describe the characteristics of geometric shapes, angles, or parallel lines.

In a social science class, this graphic organizer can be used to identify the characteristics of historical documents, important battles, or famous people in history. It can also be used to describe the characteristics of different land forms, maps, or archeological sites. How about characteristics of supply-side economics or Jungian psychology? The possibilities are endless.

In science class, this graphic organizer can be used to describe the characteristics of mammals, cells, parts of the brain, chemistry elements, or types of weather. Again, the uses of this graphic organizer are endless.

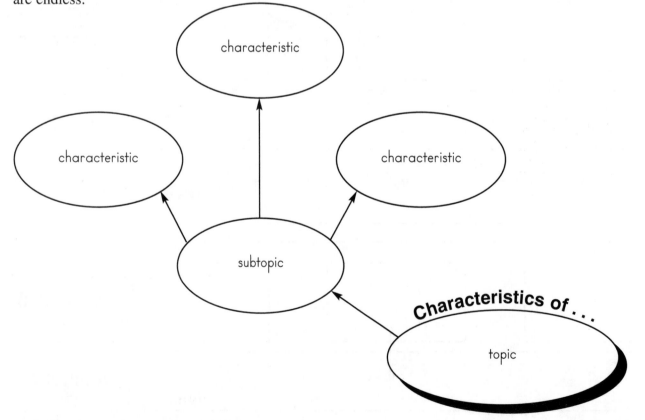

Characteristics of. . .

This example is from *Lightning* by Seymour Simon (Scholastic, 1997).

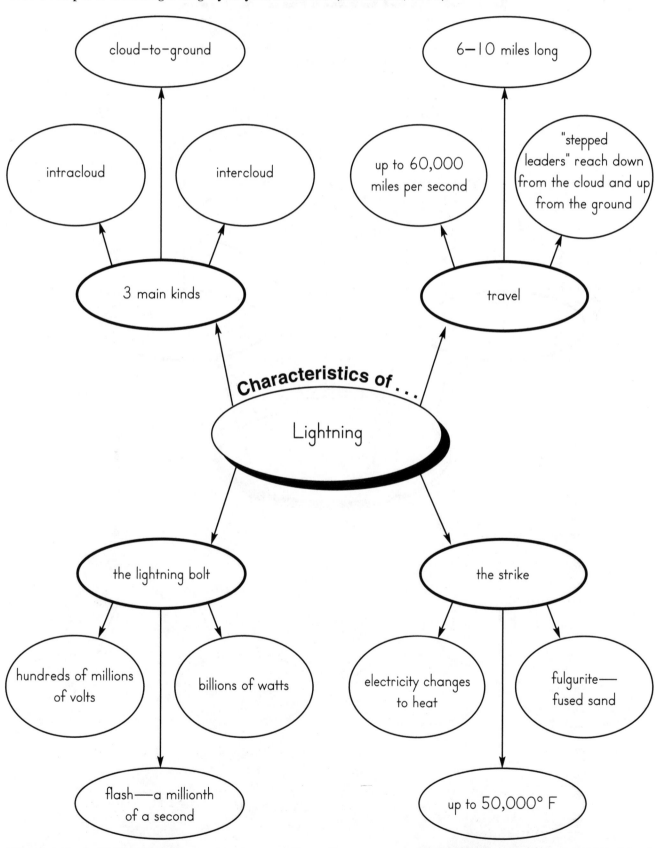

Name _____   Date _____

Characteristics of . . .

_____
(title/author)

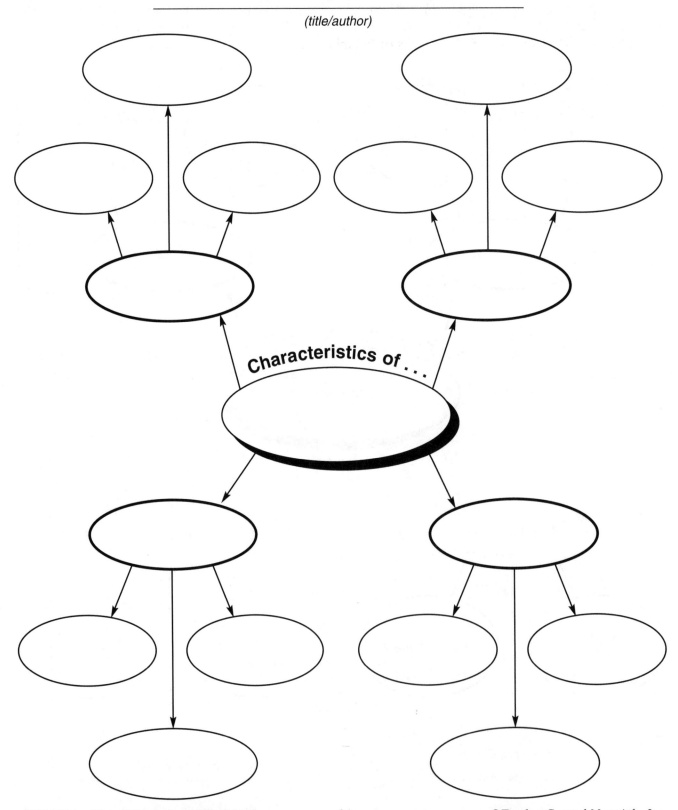

Compare and Contrast

Students can use this modified Venn diagram to identify likenesses and differences in just about anything. Use this graphic organizer in language arts to identify likenesses and differences between characters, settings, or different books by the same author. Use it in history to compare and contrast different cultures, countries, geographical features, or famous people in history. You can use it in math to compare and contrast geometrical objects, angles, or problem-solving strategies. In science, use it to compare and contrast plants, planets, types of lightning, or rocks and minerals.

Different

characteristics that are unique to item #1

Alike

characteristics item #1 and item #2 have in common

Different

characteristics that are unique to item #2

In some cases, you may want to contrast and compare three different picture books, poems, characters, settings, events, etc. The *Three-Way Compare and Contrast* graphic organizer will allow you to do this. List the details that are unique to each item in the boxes labeled *Different*. The challenge is to find details that are alike for all three items you are comparing and list them in the section labeled *Alike*.

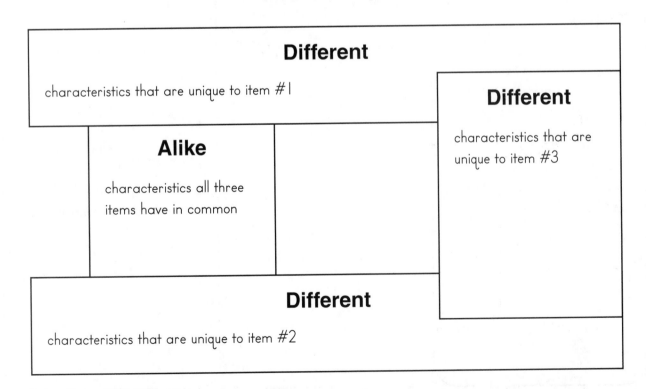

Different

characteristics that are unique to item #1

Different

characteristics that are unique to item #3

Alike

characteristics all three items have in common

Different

characteristics that are unique to item #2

Compare and Contrast

This example is from *The Amazing Life of Benjamin Franklin* by James Cross Giblin (Scholastic, 2000) and *Alexander Graham Bell* by Leonard Everett Fisher (Atheneum, 1999).

Different	Alike	Different
The Amazing Life of Benjamin Franklin	both loved the sea and wondered about it	*Alexander Graham Bell*
only 2 years of schooling	both had a sense of curiosity that moved them into the field of science and discovery	musician
involved in the printing business	both were visionaries in their own way	well educated
at 42, retired from printing and devoted time to science	both had a love of science	very interested in the human voice
involved in public and government duties	both were inventors	drawn to hearing-impaired and established a school for them
helped negotiate a peace treaty	both married and had families	founded Bell Telephone Company
delegate to convention that wrote the Constitution		generously supported the scientific endeavors of others
invented: lightning rod, Franklin stove, bifocal glasses, library chair, clock with three wheels, "artificial arm"		invented: telephone, metal detector, spectra phone, vacuum jacket, electrical devices to assist the deaf, perfected the "hydrofoil"

Three-Way Compare and Contrast

The picture books used in this example are *The Korean Cinderella* by Shirley Climo (HarperCollins, 1993); *The Turkey Girl, A Zuni Cinderella Story* by Penny Pollock (Little Brown and Company, 1996); and *Cendrillon, A Caribbean Cinderella* by Robert D. San Souci (Alladin Paperbacks, 1998).

Different

Cendrillon, A Caribbean Cinderella

lives in the Caribbean

stepmother makes her a serving girl

loses her slipper at the ball

Paul looks for her, using her slipper

marries the handsome Paul

Different

Turkey Girl, A Zuni Cinderella Story

has no family at all

lives somewhere in the desert

cares for the turkeys

leaves the dance too late

turkeys leave her because she does not keep her promise

Alike

young girls whose mothers have died

go to a type of dance

wear rags for clothes

had to work very hard

someone or something helps them so they can attend the dance

Different

The Korean Cinderella

stepmother makes her do all of the work

chores are impossible to do

animals help her accomplish the impossible tasks

loses her sandal in the water

magistrate looks for her with the sandal

marries the magistrate

Name _____   Date _____

Compare and Contrast

Different	Alike	Different

Name _____   Date _____

Three-Way Compare and Contrast

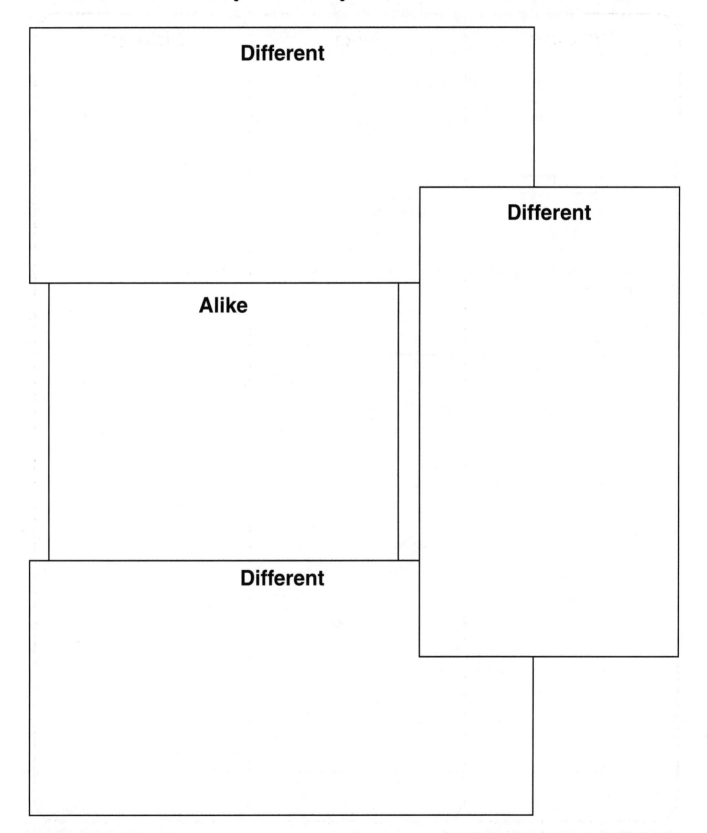

Different

Different

Alike

Different

Fact, Fiction, or Opinion?

Picture books contain a variety of facts, fiction, and opinions. No matter which picture book you choose, your students should be able to identify facts that the author uses in the story. Have students look closely at the setting, characters, and plot of the story, remembering that facts are statements that can be proven. As they are reading or listening to a story, students should decide if "this could really happen." Students should list facts in the section of the organizer labeled *Just the Facts!*

In the section labeled *Fiction or Opinion*, students should list anything that is not fact. Many picture books feature talking animals, imaginary settings, or fantastic events that are clearly not real. Some authors, however, skillfully mix fact and fiction, and students may have to look very closely to tell the difference.

When looking for opinions, have students pay special attention to what the characters say as they move through the story. Students should be able to pick out opinions expressed by the characters by looking for statements that cannot be proven. You can also use the opinions side of this graphic organizer to have students list their own opinions of the characters, decisions, actions, and results in the story. Then, have students summarize their opinions at the bottom of the graphic organizer. If you use this as a response to literature, students will learn how to form an opinion of a story and compare opinions with their classmates.

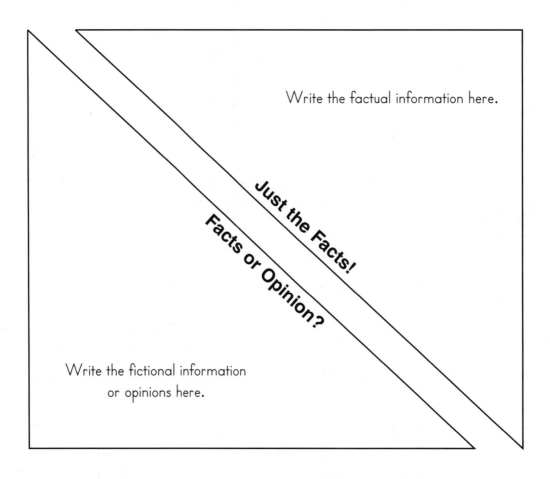

Fact, Fiction, or Opinion?

This example is from *Sir Cumference and the Great Knight of Angleland* by Cindy Neuschwander (Charlesbridge, 1997).

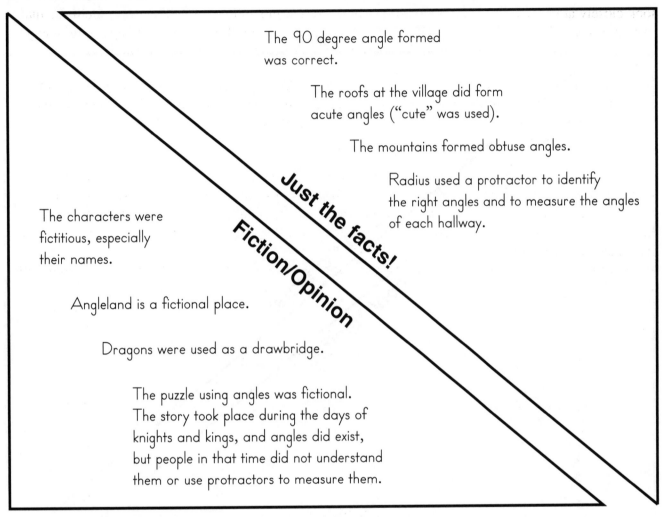

The 90 degree angle formed was correct.

The roofs at the village did form acute angles ("cute" was used).

The mountains formed obtuse angles.

Radius used a protractor to identify the right angles and to measure the angles of each hallway.

Just the facts!

Fiction/Opinion

The characters were fictitious, especially their names.

Angleland is a fictional place.

Dragons were used as a drawbridge.

The puzzle using angles was fictional. The story took place during the days of knights and kings, and angles did exist, but people in that time did not understand them or use protractors to measure them.

How does the author weave fact, fiction, and/or opinion together to make the selection more interesting?

The story was fiction because the characters, setting, and plot are all fictional. However, the author

used interesting names for the characters (Radius, Sir Cumference, Lady Di of Ameter, Sir D'Grees)

that are based on math terms. These characters and the use of angles to solve the problem of the lost

king made the story a mathematical adventure.

Name _____   Date _____

Fact, Fiction, or Opinion?

_____
(title/author)

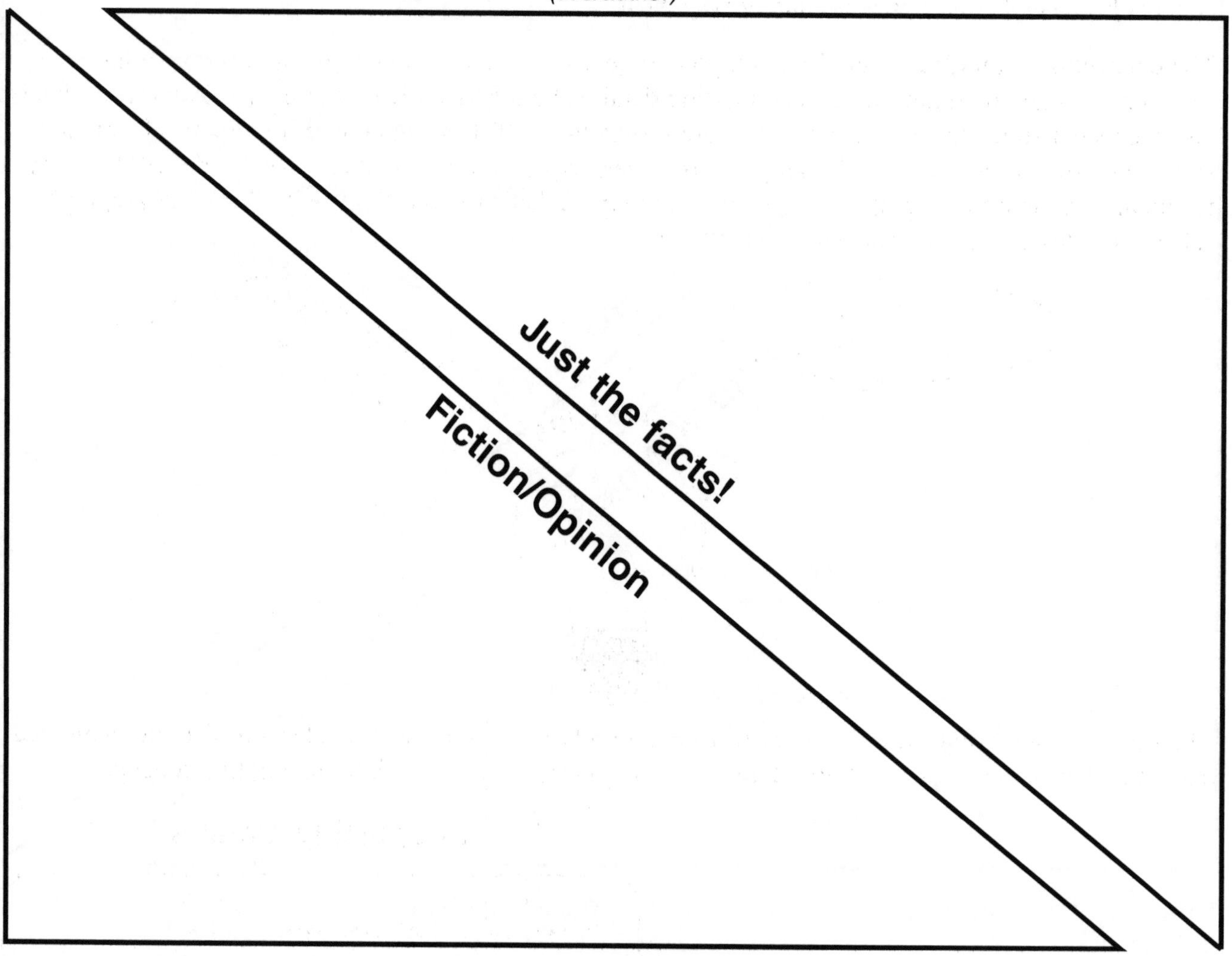

Just the facts!

Fiction/Opinion

How does the author weave fact, fiction, and/or opinions together to make the selection more interesting? _____

_____

_____

_____

_____

Main Idea and Supporting Details

The main idea and supporting details of a text are sometimes tough for students to identify. The use of picture books and graphic organizers can make it easier for students to learn this concept. Some texts have a main idea that is easy for students to grasp, while others may have an inferred main idea that makes it more difficult to identify. Nonfiction picture books are excellent for introducing the use of this concept because the main idea is usually very clear.

The concept of main idea is helpful when you are teaching students how to paraphrase or summarize. They must locate the main idea and supporting details of a text and then write their summaries. This is also a concept students can use when they are researching. If they can choose important information and summarize it on this type of a graphic organizer, writing a report in their own words will be easier for them. The main idea graphic organizers can help students focus on the main idea of a paragraph, selection of text, or even a chapter of a textbook.

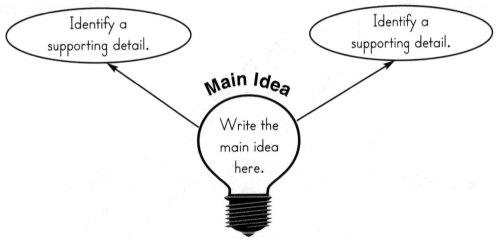

The first graphic organizer, titled *Main Idea*, is a simple version that asks students to list one main idea and a number of supporting details. This is a good place to start when introducing this concept.

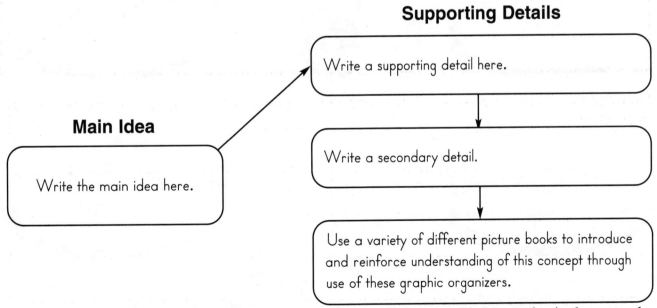

The second organizer, titled *Main Idea and Supporting Details*, is a little more complex in that not only are the main idea and supporting details identified, but secondary details are identified as well.

Main Idea

The picture book *Albert* by Donna Jo Napoli (Harcourt, 2001) was used for this example.

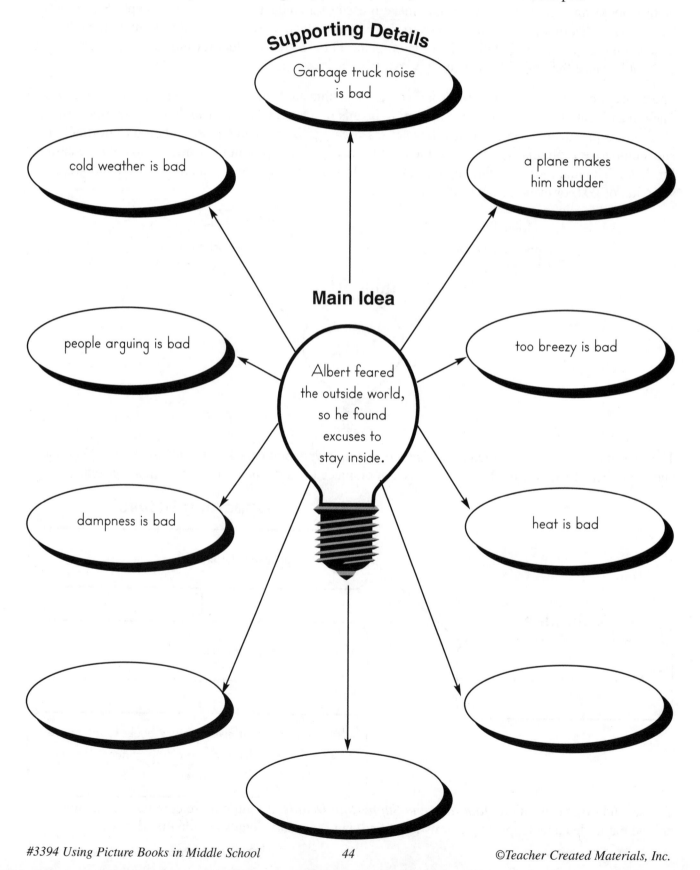

Supporting Details

Garbage truck noise is bad

cold weather is bad

a plane makes him shudder

Main Idea

people arguing is bad

Albert feared the outside world, so he found excuses to stay inside.

too breezy is bad

dampness is bad

heat is bad

44

Main Idea and Supporting Details

The picture book *How Turtle's Back Was Cracked*, retold by Gayle Ross (Dial Books, 1995), was used for this example.

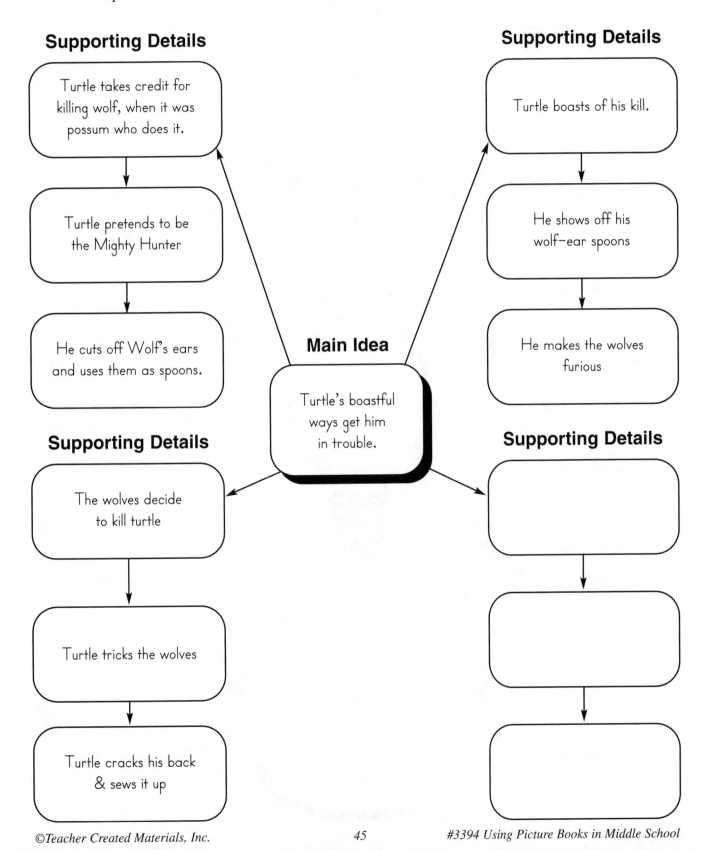

Supporting Details

Turtle takes credit for killing wolf, when it was possum who does it.

Turtle pretends to be the Mighty Hunter

He cuts off Wolf's ears and uses them as spoons.

Supporting Details

The wolves decide to kill turtle

Turtle tricks the wolves

Turtle cracks his back & sews it up

Main Idea

Turtle's boastful ways get him in trouble.

Supporting Details

Turtle boasts of his kill.

He shows off his wolf-ear spoons

He makes the wolves furious

Supporting Details

Name _____   Date _____

Main Idea

_____
(title/author)

Supporting Details

Main Idea

Name _____   Date _____

Main Idea

_____
(title/author)

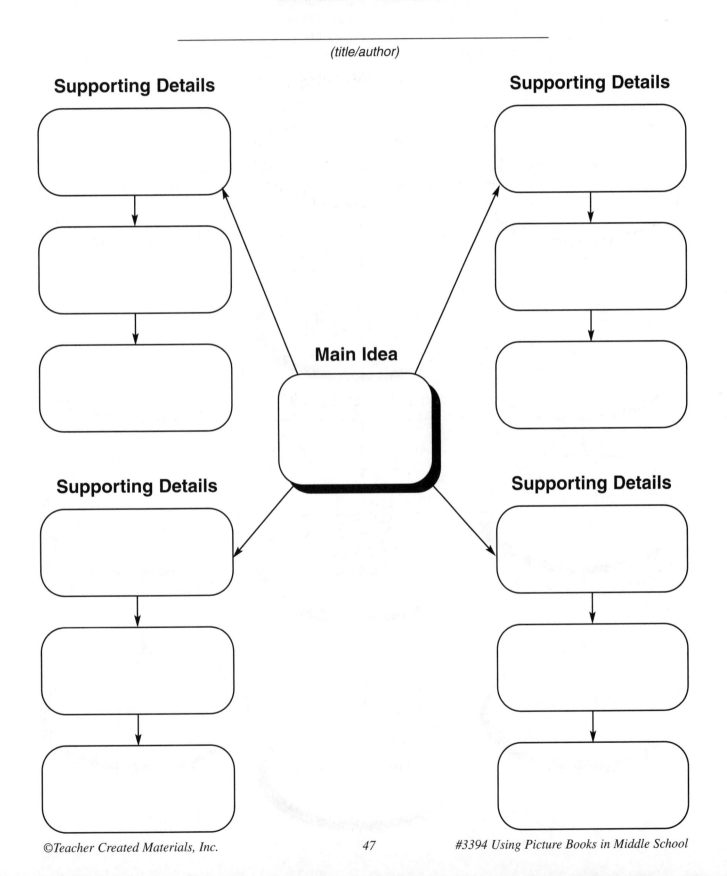

Supporting Details

Supporting Details

Main Idea

Supporting Details

Supporting Details

Mood, Feelings, and Attitudes

This organizer helps students identify how an author conveys mood, feelings, and/or attitudes through the characters, setting, and plot of a story. In some cases, students get so caught up in the story that they don't stop to think about how the author sets up the feelings and attitudes of the characters and how these affect the mood of the story. Picture books are ideal for teaching this concept since they are typically short enough to allow students to pick out these characteristics. Read a variety of picture books with your students so they can learn to identify different moods and feelings.

Some picture books create happy feelings by making you laugh at the characters' actions. In other picture books, the mood is more serious because the plot of the story involves serious issues and events. In these stories, the author may create a mood of sadness, grief, or depression through the characters and what happens to them. Having your students analyze the elements of a story will help them realize how the main idea, character development, and supporting details work together to create the mood of a story.

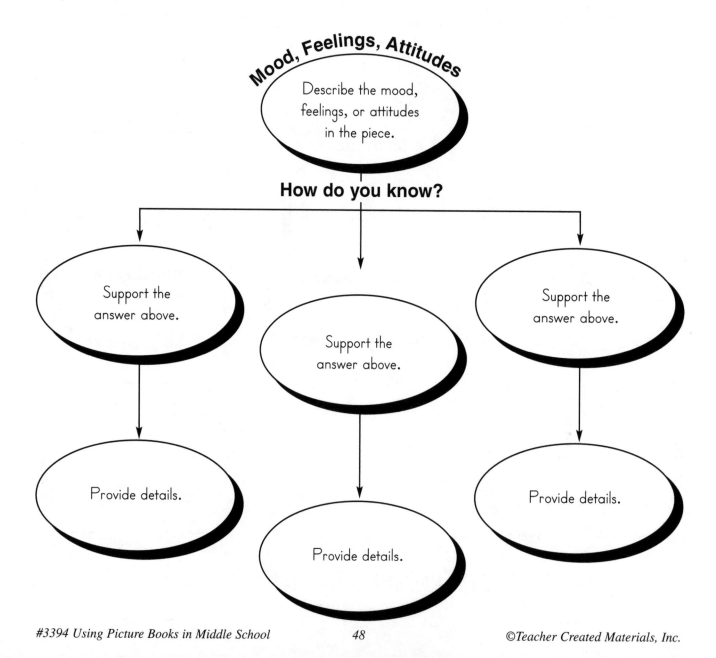

Mood/Feelings/Attitude

This example comes from *Feathers and Fools* by Mem Fox (Harcourt, Inc., 1989).

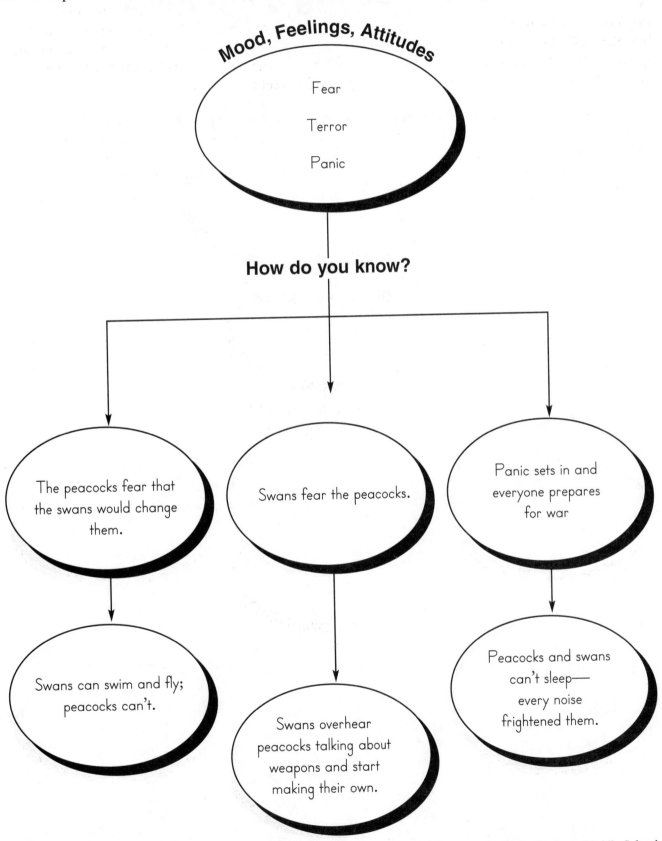

Mood, Feelings, Attitudes

Fear

Terror

Panic

How do you know?

The peacocks fear that the swans would change them.

Swans fear the peacocks.

Panic sets in and everyone prepares for war

Swans can swim and fly; peacocks can't.

Swans overhear peacocks talking about weapons and start making their own.

Peacocks and swans can't sleep— every noise frightened them.

Name _____   Date _____

Mood, Feelings, Attitudes

_____

(title/author)

Mood, Feelings, Attitudes

How do you know?

Plot

Students can use this graphic organizer to identify the rising action, climax, and resolution of a story. As you read a picture book to your students, have them identify the climax of the story. This is the most important event that usually takes place toward the end of a story. Once they have identified the climax, have them work backwards to identify the rising action that leads up to the climax. Then, have them identify the resolution that follows the climax and finishes the story.

Read a variety of picture books to help students understand how different authors set up the rising action, climax, and resolution in their stories. Practicing this concept with picture books will help your students realize how important plot is in a good story that keeps the reader's attention. Students will then be able to transfer this knowledge of story structure to their own writing.

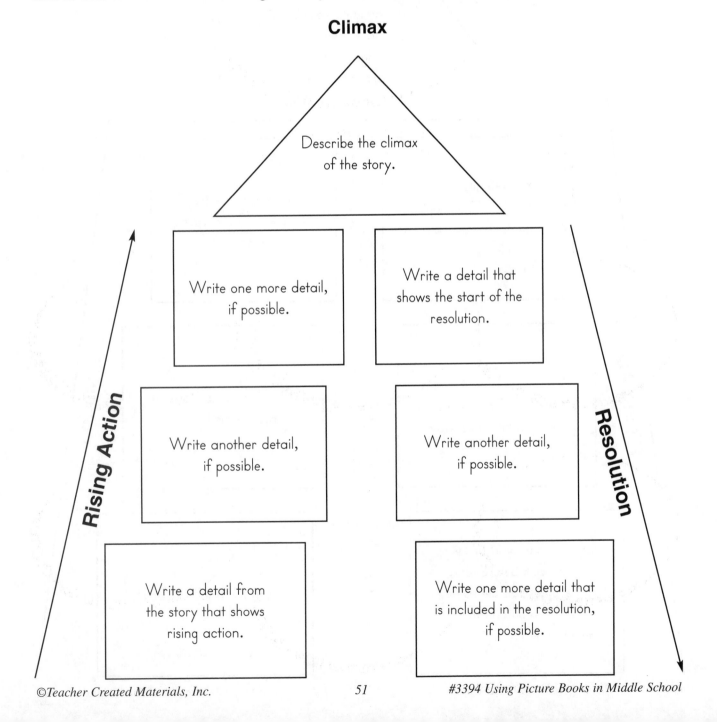

Plot

This example is from *The Magic Fan* by Keith Baker (Harcourt Brace, 1989).

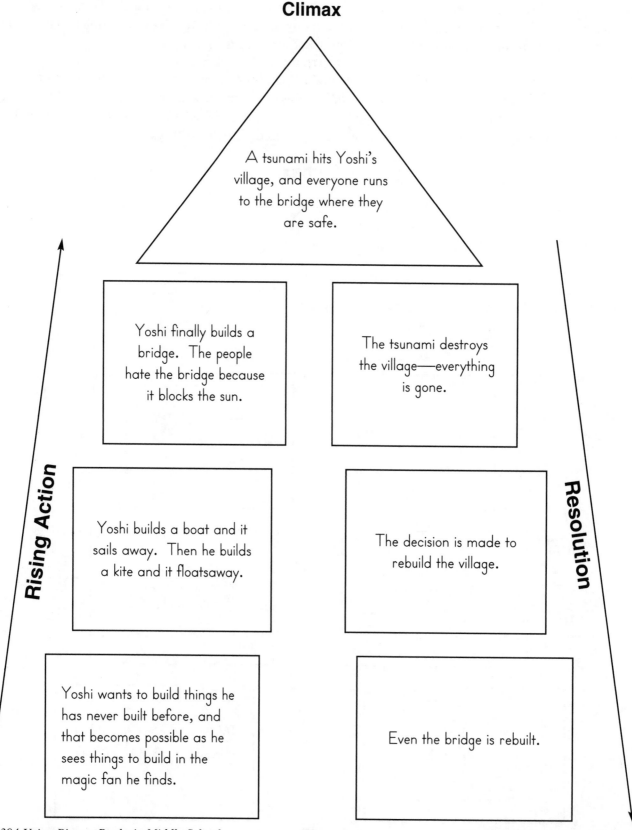

Climax

A tsunami hits Yoshi's village, and everyone runs to the bridge where they are safe.

Rising Action

Yoshi finally builds a bridge. The people hate the bridge because it blocks the sun.

The tsunami destroys the village—everything is gone.

Yoshi builds a boat and it sails away. Then he builds a kite and it floatsaway.

The decision is made to rebuild the village.

Yoshi wants to build things he has never built before, and that becomes possible as he sees things to build in the magic fan he finds.

Even the bridge is rebuilt.

Resolution

Name _____   Date _____

Plot

_____
(title/author)

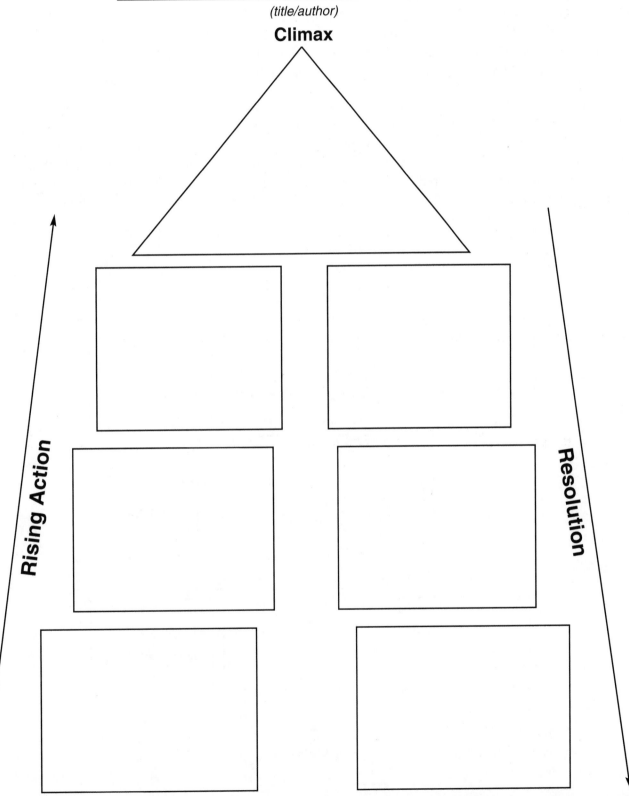

Climax

Rising Action

Resolution

Predictions

Predictions keep students alert and thinking ahead as a story is read to them. As you are reading a picture book to your students, pause every once in a while and ask students to predict what will happen. If students are reading to themselves, ask them to pause and predict every few pages.

You can customize the *Predictions* graphic organizer with the predictions you want your students to make. For example, if you want students to predict the end of the story, simply write "Predict the Ending of the Story" in the center box. In the surrounding boxes, students can write the story details and/or background knowledge that led them to their prediction.

You can also use this graphic organizer to have students predict what will and will not happen in the story. The organizer has been designed with three supporting detail boxes on top and three on the bottom. Draw a horizontal line through the prediction box in the middle and write the phrase "What Will Happen" in the top half of the box and write "What Will Not Happen" in the bottom half of the middle box. Students fill the top three boxes with details supporting their predictions of what will happen, and in the bottom three boxes they write details supporting their predictions of what will not happen.

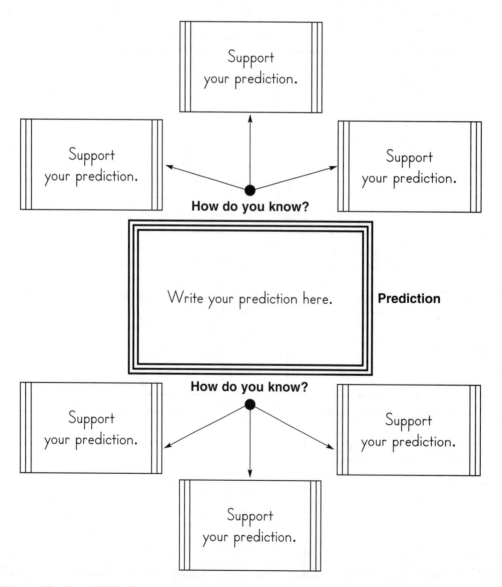

Predictions

The following example is taken from the book *The Sea Chest* by Toni Buzzeo (Dial Books, 2002).

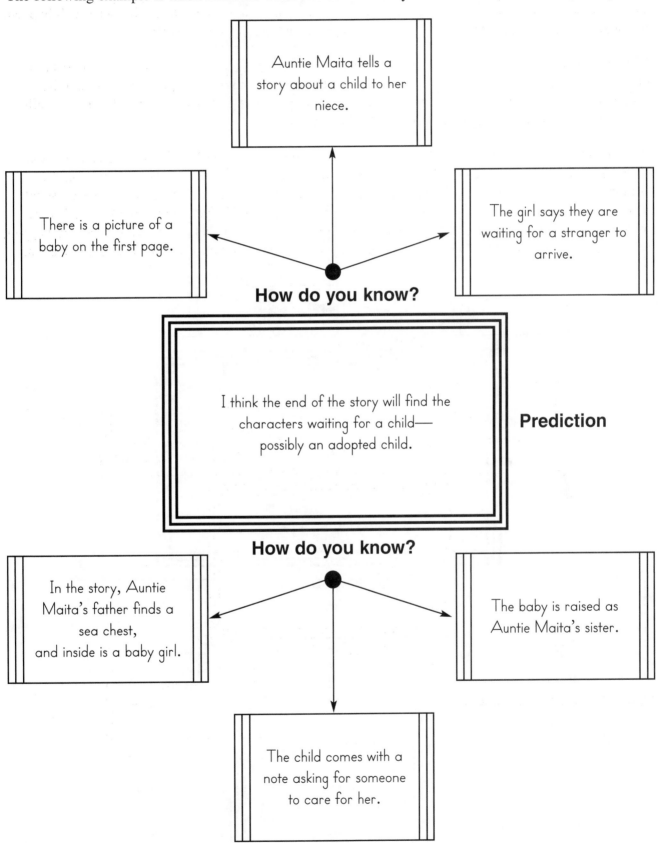

Auntie Maita tells a story about a child to her niece.

There is a picture of a baby on the first page.

The girl says they are waiting for a stranger to arrive.

How do you know?

I think the end of the story will find the characters waiting for a child—possibly an adopted child.

Prediction

How do you know?

In the story, Auntie Maita's father finds a sea chest, and inside is a baby girl.

The baby is raised as Auntie Maita's sister.

The child comes with a note asking for someone to care for her.

Name _____   Date _____

Predictions

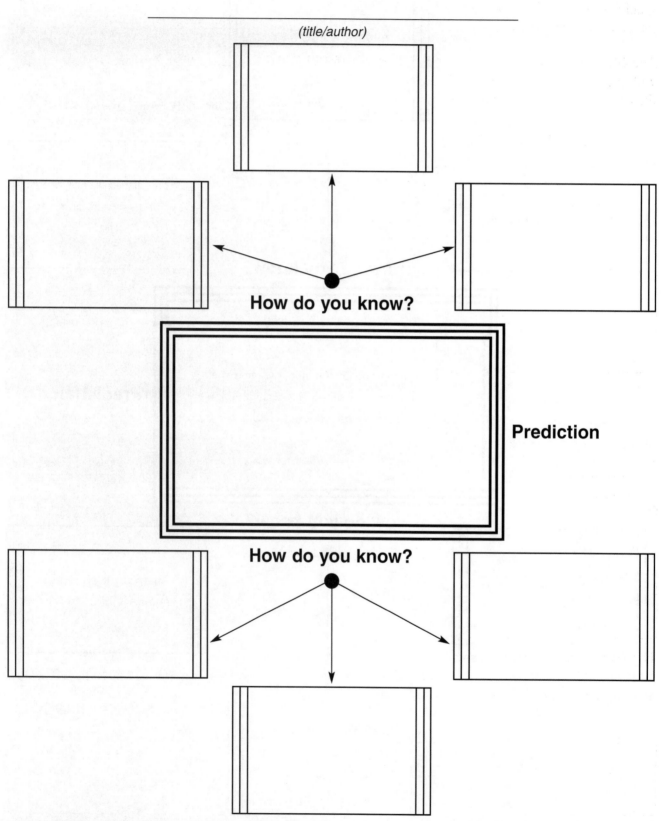

_____
(title/author)

How do you know?

Prediction

How do you know?

Sequencing

Students can use these organizers to define the sequence of events after a book is read to them, in the content areas during research, or in math to identify a sequence of steps. There are several different graphic organizers to choose from for this concept. You can have students choose the one they would rather work with, or you can choose the one that best fits your needs.

The *Graphic Sequencing* organizer will work best for those students who like to express their thoughts with pictures. Students have the freedom to draw scenes that represent the sequence of the story and then add captions to describe the events.

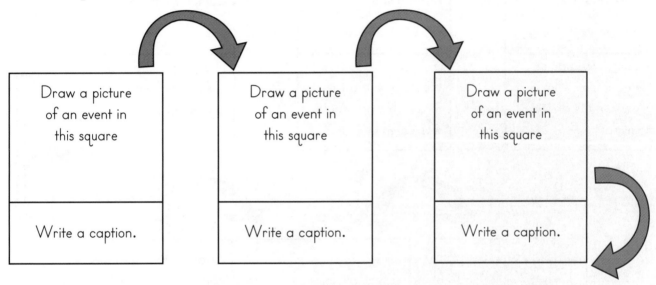

The *Beginning, Middle, and End* graphic organizer gives students the ability to see the "whole picture" of the story and break it into pieces. All of the events in these three parts of a story should be included.

Beginning	**Middle**	**End**
Write all of the important events that take place in the beginning of the story.	Write all of the important events that take place in the middle of the story.	Write all of the important events that take place at the end of the story.

The *Timeline* sequencing organizer can be used to sequence events in a story or steps in a math problem, or it can be used as a timeline in other subject areas. Use the small box in the corner to identify the date, day, or number of the event or step.

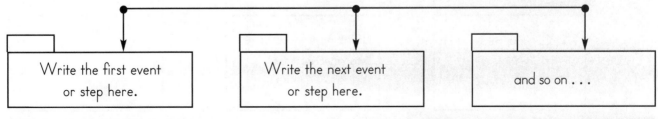

Graphic Sequencing

This example is from *The Story of Jumping Mouse* by John Steptoe (Lothrop, Lee, 1972).

Draw a picture of a mouse and a frog.	Draw a picture of a fat mouse and a snake.	Draw a picture of Jumping Mouse and a buffalo.
Magic Frog names him Jumping Mouse & gives him the ability to jump.	He stays with a fat mouse, but fat mouse was eaten by a snake.	Jumping Mouse gives buffalo the ability to see, and he goes blind.

Draw a picture of Jumping Mouse and Magic Frog together.	Draw a picture of Jumping Mouse crying.	Draw a picture of the blind Jumping Mouse and the wolf.
Magic Frog appears and reassures Jumping Mouse that he'll be okay.	Jumping Mouse arrives at destination, but is sad.	Jumping Mouse gives wolf the ability to smell, and looses his.

 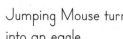

Draw a picture of Jumping Mouse jumping high into the air.	Draw a picture of Jumping Mouse turning into an eagle.	
Magic Frog tells Jumping Mouse to jump high.	Jumping Mouse turns into an eagle.	

Beginning, Middle, and End

This example is from the picture book *Frightful's Daughter* by Jean Craighead George (Dutton, 2002).

Beginning

Frightful hatches three peregrine falcon chicks.

Oksi is the one who does things her way—and it always seems to be the opposite of what was expected.

When warned of danger Oksi backs into the shadow of her home, while her brothers flatten themselves and remain still.

Middle

Her brothers are stolen by a falcon thief, and her actions save her—but Frightful doesn't know that.

Sam sees the whole thing and takes Oksi home to the forest.

Oksi's mother does finally find her.

Sam helps by feeding them as Oksi grows.

When it comes time to migrate, Oksi stays behind.

Sam has to care for her through the winter.

End

Spring arrives, and Oksi leaves for her hunting grounds along the river.

Sam thinks for sure he will never see her again.

One day, Oksi shows up to the perch where she was raised, and Falco, a male peregrine falcon, joins her.

Sam is looking forward to new baby peregrine falcons.

Timeline

This example is from the book *Building A New Land, African Americans in Colonial America* by James Haskins and Kathleen Benson (Harper Collins, 2001).

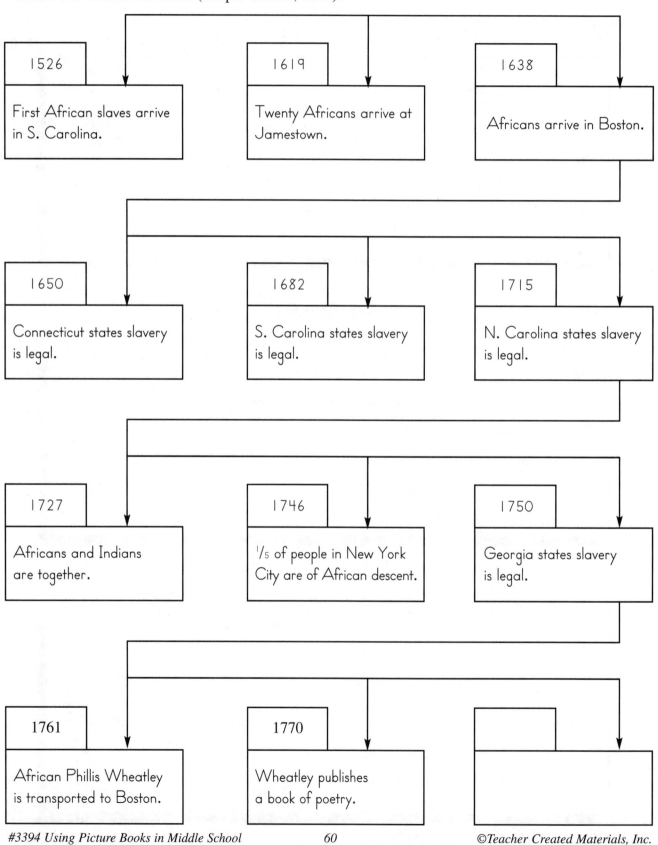

1526	1619	1638
First African slaves arrive in S. Carolina.	Twenty Africans arrive at Jamestown.	Africans arrive in Boston.

1650	1682	1715
Connecticut states slavery is legal.	S. Carolina states slavery is legal.	N. Carolina states slavery is legal.

1727	1746	1750
Africans and Indians are together.	1/5 of people in New York City are of African descent.	Georgia states slavery is legal.

1761	1770	
African Phillis Wheatley is transported to Boston.	Wheatley publishes a book of poetry.	

Name _____   Date _____

Sequencing

_____
(title/author)

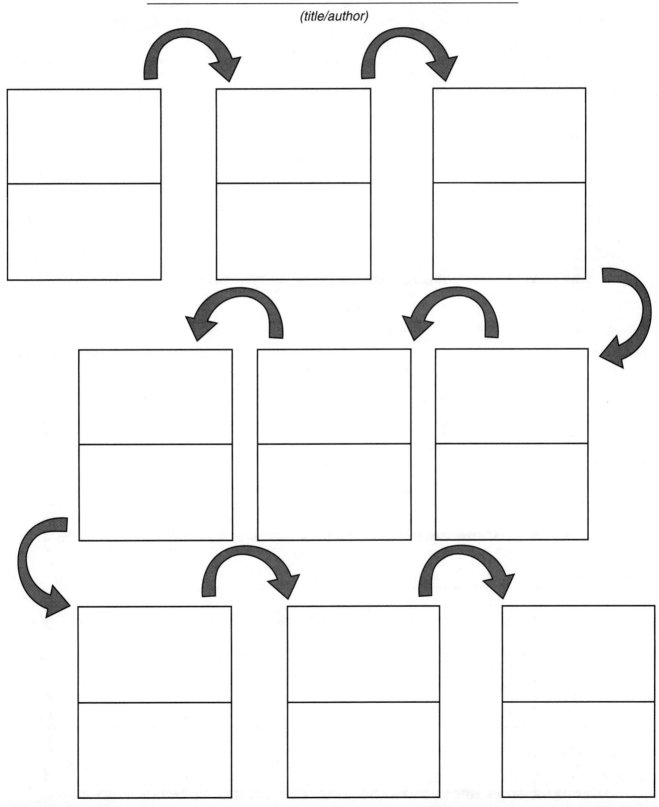

Name _____   Date _____

Beginning, Middle, and End

_____
(title/author)

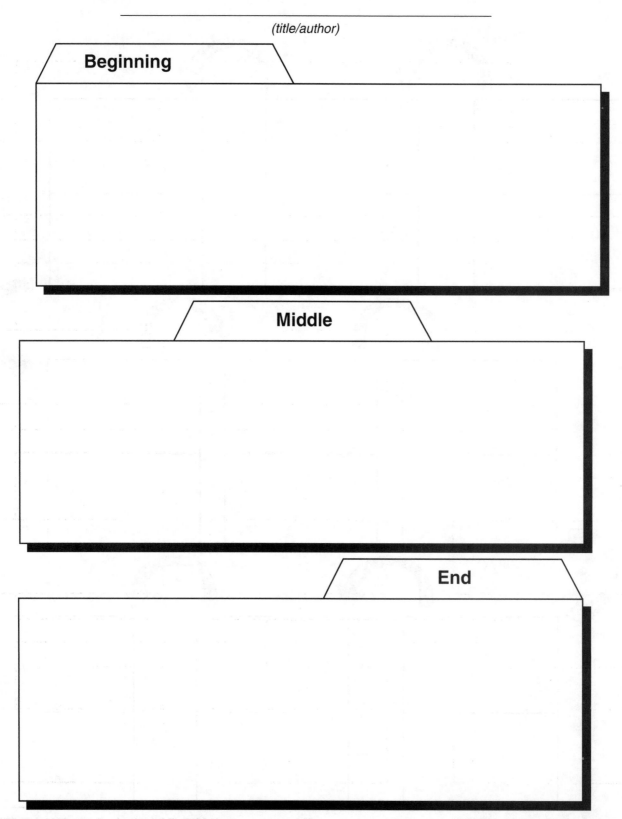

Beginning

Middle

End

Name _____   Date _____

Sequencing

_____
(title/author)

Setting

Too often students overlook the importance of the setting in a piece of writing. These graphic organizers will help students become aware of the presence of the setting, the way the author describes the setting, and the purpose of the setting.

The graphic organizer titled *Setting Description* asks students to look carefully at the author's description of the setting. Read several different books by different authors to give students a deeper understanding of the different ways authors can describe a setting.

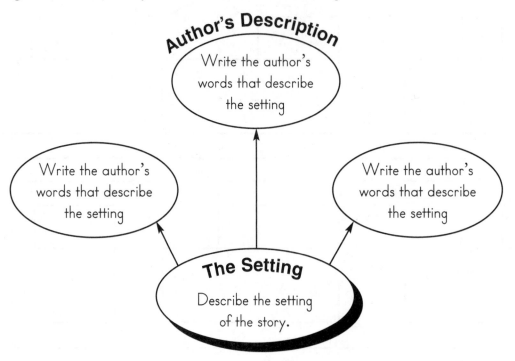

The graphic organizer titled *Effects of the Setting* helps students examine how the setting affects the story. After students have filled out this graphic organizer, ask them how changing the setting would affect the story.

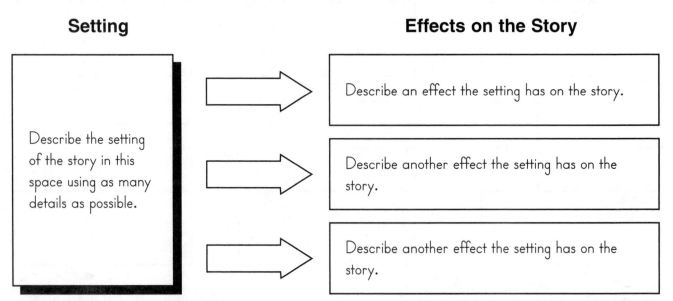

Setting Description

When filling in this graphic organizer, students look for specific words or phrases that the author uses to describe the setting. This example is from *The Legend of the Loon* by Kathy-jo Wargin (Sleeping Bear, 2000).

Author's Description

Many lakes, wooded land

spring—a garden of lady slippers and ferns

summer—pines and cedars reflect on the water

The Setting

Northern Michigan

winter—a land of frost and mist

sky-blue lake, stone cliffs, small bay

autumn—a wild feast of color and sound

Effects of the Setting

This example is from *Angels in the Dust* by Margot Theis Raven (Bridgewater, 2002).

Setting   ## Effects on the Story

The story takes place on a farm in the Panhandle plains of Oklahoma.

The family make their living by growing wheat on flat farmland.

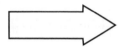

The story takes place in the Dust Bowl. Several times the story talks about the great dust storms that move through this area.

The drought makes it difficult, if not impossible, to grow crops and make a future for the family. Dust storms and hot winds dry out crops and soil.

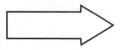

The story takes place during the Depression.

No one has much to speak of, but they make do with what they have. Everyone has to stick together in order to survive.

Name _____   Date _____

Setting Description

_____
(title/author)

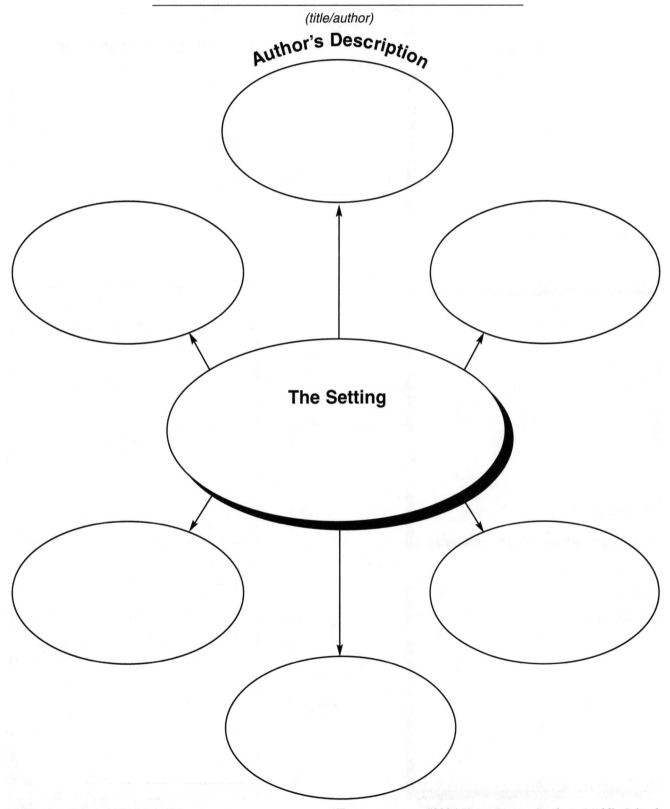

Author's Description

The Setting

Name _____   Date _____

Effects of the Setting

_____
(title/author)

Setting   **Effects on the Story**

Vocabulary

Two different graphic organizers are provided to help students understand parts of speech, learn new word definitions, and examine how authors use vocabulary to make their stories more interesting.

The first organizer, *Descriptive Vocabulary*, asks students to identify the adjectives, adverbs, and verbs that an author uses to make a story interesting. Too often, students get stuck using the same words for describing action or dialogue. As students identify verbs, adverbs, and adjectives and how to use them, have them each keep an ongoing list that will provide them with the words they need to help liven up their own writing.

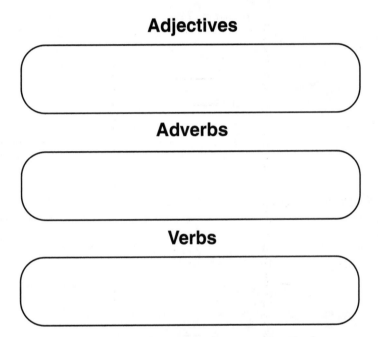

Adjectives

Adverbs

Verbs

This graphic organizer, *New Vocabulary*, can be used as an ongoing list of new words, their meanings, and examples of how to use them. This graphic organizer will help students use quality words properly.

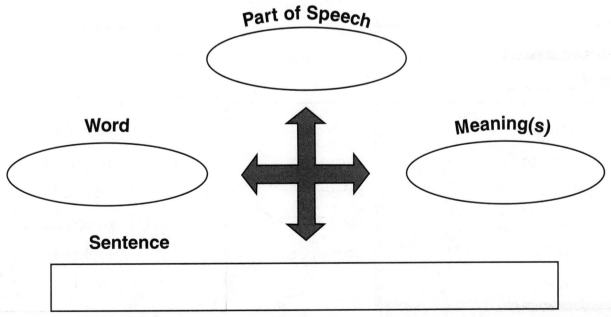

Part of Speech

Word

Meaning(s)

Sentence

Descriptive Vocabulary

This example is from *The Shaman's Apprentice* by Lynne Cherry and Mark J. Plotkin (Harcourt, Inc., 1998).

Adjectives

beautiful	plastic	healing
powerful	emerald	white
metal pots	scarlet	medicinal
poison	patient	wise

Adverbs

gently	soon	deep
softly	free	nearby
silently	effortlessly	beside
sadly	carefully	

Verbs

burning	hunted	exchanged
whispered	swam	sustained
carried	fished	believed
removed	convert	accompanied
harvested	unwrapped	explained
arrived		

New Vocabulary

This example is from *The Alamo* by Shelley Tanaka (Madison Press, 2003).

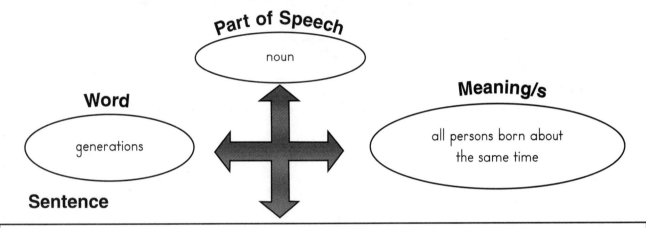

Part of Speech
noun

Word
generations

Meaning/s
all persons born about the same time

Sentence

There were many generations of families that moved west for gold, farming, and ranching.

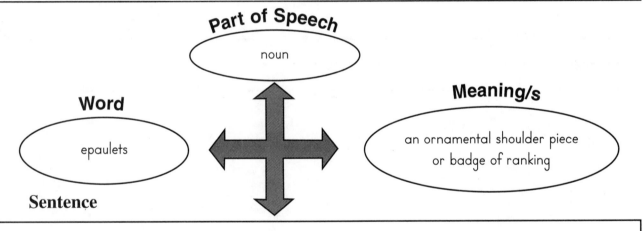

Part of Speech
noun

Word
epaulets

Meaning/s
an ornamental shoulder piece or badge of ranking

Sentence

The Mexican president looked magnificent as his gold epaulets gleamed in the sunlight.

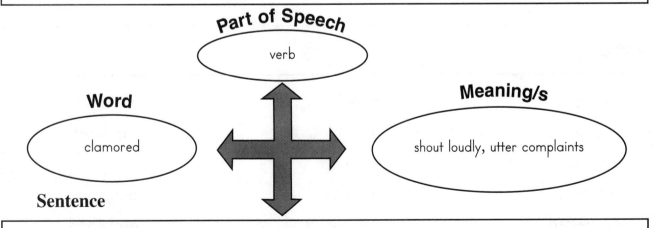

Part of Speech
verb

Word
clamored

Meaning/s
shout loudly, utter complaints

Sentence

As the battle progressed, men clamored as they climbed over bodies of their fellow soldiers.

Name _____   Date _____

Descriptive Vocabulary

_____
(title/author)

Adjectives

Adverbs

Verbs

Name _____   Date _____

New Vocabulary

_____
(title/author)

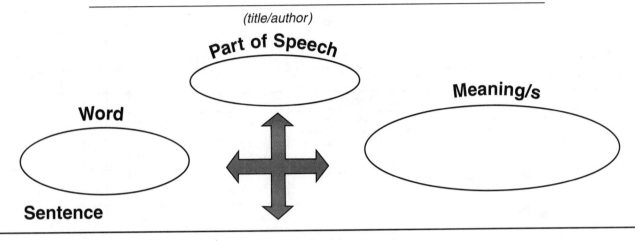

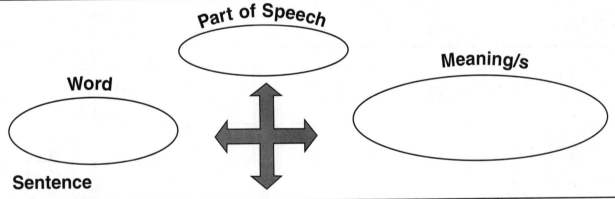

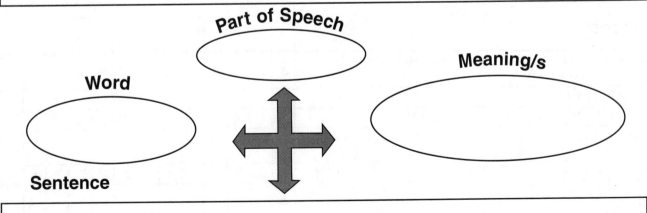

Bibliography Grid

	Cause & Effect	Character Analysis	Characteristics of . . .	Compare & Contrast	Fact, Fiction, or Opinion?	Main Idea	Mood/Feelings/Attitudes	Plot	Predictions	Sequencing	Setting	Vocabulary	Partner Books
Animals													
Frightful's Daughter by Jean Craighead George. Dutton, 2002.	X	X	X	X	X	X	X	X	X	X	X	X	
Frightful's Mountain by Jean Craighead George. Puffin, 2001.	X	X	X	X	X	X	X	X	X	X	X	X	X
Julie of the Wolves by Jean Craighead George. Harper Trophy, 2003.	X	X	X	X	X	X	X	X	X	X	X	X	
Once A Wolf. . . by Stephen R. Swinburne. Houghton Mifflin, 1999.	X			X	X	X	X			X	X		
Series: *Silverwing,* 1999; *Sunwing,* 2001; *Firewing,* 2003. Simon & Schuster	X	X	X	X	X	X	X	X	X	X	X	X	
Stellaluna by Janell Cannon. Scholastic Inc., 1993.	X	X	X	X	X	X	X	X	X	X	X	X	
The Last Lobo by Roland Smith. Hyperion Books, 1999.	X	X	X	X	X	X	X	X	X	X	X	X	X
The Story of Jumping Mouse by John Steptoe. Lothrop, Lee, 1972.	X	X	X	X	X	X	X	X	X	X	X	X	
Verdi by Janell Cannon. Harcourt Brace, 1997.	X	X	X	X	X	X	X	X	X	X	X	X	
Wolves by Gail Gibbons. Holiday House, 1994.	X	X		X	X	X	X		X		X	X	
Biographies													
Alexander Graham Bell by Leonard Everett Fisher. Atheneum, 1999.	X	X	X	X		X	X		X	X		X	
The Amazing Life of Benjamin Franklin by James Cross Giblin. Scholastic, 2000.	X	X	X	X		X	X		X	X		X	
George Washington: A Picture Book Biography by James Cross Giblin. Scholastic, 1992.	X	X	X	X	X	X	X	X	X	X	X	X	
Lincoln: A Photobiography by Russell Freedman. Clarion, 1987.	X	X	X	X	X	X	X	X	X	X	X	X	X
Talkin' Bout Bess: The Story of Aviator Bessie Coleman by Nikki Grimes. Scholastic, 2003.	X	X	X	X		X	X		X	X		X	
The Revolutionary John Adams by Cheryl Harness. National Geographic, 2003.	X	X	X	X		X	X		X	X		X	
Thomas Jefferson: A Picture Book Biography by James Cross Giblin. Scholastic, 1994.	X	X	X	X		X	X		X	X		X	
Cinderella Tales													
Adelita by Tomie dePaola. G.P. Putnam, 2002.	X	X	X	X		X		X		X	X	X	
Cendrillon: A Caribbean Cinderella by Robert D. San Souci. Alladdin Paperbacks, 1998.	X	X	X	X		X		X		X	X	X	
The Egyptian Cinderella by Shirley Climo. HarperCollins, 1989.	X	X	X	X		X		X		X	X	X	
The Gift of the Crocodile by Judy Sierra. Simon & Schuster, 2000.	X	X	X	X		X		X		X	X	X	
The Korean Cinderella by Shirley Climo. HarperCollins, 1993.	X	X	X	X		X	X	X		X	X	X	
The Persian Cinderella by Shirley Climo. HarperCollins, 1999.	X	X	X	X		X	X	X		X	X	X	

Bibliography Grid *(cont.)*

	Cause & Effect	Character Analysis	Characteristics of . . .	Compare & Contrast	Fact, Fiction, or Opinion?	Main Idea	Mood/Feelings/Attitudes	Plot	Predictions	Sequencing	Setting	Vocabulary	Partner Books
The Rough-Face Girl by Rafe Martin. Scholastic Inc., 1992.	X	X	X	X		X		X		X	X	X	
The Turkey Girl: A Zuni Cinderella Story by Penny Pollock. Little Brown and Company, 1996.	X	X	X	X		X		X		X	X	X	
Yeh-Shen: A Cinderella Story from China by Louie Ai-Ling. Sandcastle Books, 1982.	X	X	X	X		X		X		X	X	X	
Ecosystems/Biomes/Environment													
Alejandro's Gift by Richard E. Albert. Chronicle Books, 1994.	X	X	X		X	X	X	X	X	X	X	X	
A River Ran Wild by Lynne Cherry. Harcourt, 1992.	X		X	X	X	X	X	X	X	X	X	X	
Brother Eagle, Sister Sky by Chief Seattle. Scholastic, 1996.	X		X	X	X	X	X	X	X	X	X	X	
Jaguarundi by Virginia Hamilton. The Blue Sky Press, 1995.	X			X	X	X	X	X	X	X	X	X	
My Side of the Mountain by Jean Craighead George. Scholastic, 1988.	X	X	X	X	X	X	X	X	X	X	X	X	
Saguaro Moon: A Desert Journal by Kristin Joy Pratt-Serafini. Dawn Publications, 2002.	X		X	X	X	X		X	X	X	X	X	
The Great Kapok Tree by Lynne Cherry. Scholastic, 1990.	X		X	X	X	X	X	X	X	X	X	X	
The Shaman's Apprentice by Lynne Cherry and Mark J. Plotkin. Harcourt, Inc., 1998.	X	X	X	X	X	X	X	X	X	X	X	X	
Fiction													
A Single Shard by Linda Sue Park. Yearling Books, 2003.	X	X	X	X	X	X	X	X	X	X	X	X	
Albert by Donna Jo Napoli. Harcourt, 2001.	X	X	X	X		X	X	X	X	X	X	X	
Caught by the Sea by Gary Paulsen. Random House, 2001.	X	X	X	X	X	X	X	X	X	X	X	X	
Crickwing by Janell Cannon. Harcourt, 2000.	X	X	X	X	X	X	X	X	X	X	X	X	
Diary of a Worm by Doreen Cronin. Joanna Cotler Books, 2003.		X	X	X	X	X		X		X		X	
Going Home by Eve Bunting. HarperCollins, 1996.		X		X	X	X	X	X	X	X	X	X	
Mr. Lincoln's Way by Patricia Polacco. Philomel Books, 2001.	X	X	X	X	X	X	X	X	X	X	X	X	
Nothing But The Truth: A Documentary Novel by Avi. Avon Books, 1991.	X	X	X	X	X	X	X	X	X	X	X	X	X
Peppe the Lamplighter by Elisa Bartone. Lothrop, Lee, 1993.	X	X	X	X	X	X	X	X	X	X	X	X	
Raising Yoder's Barn by Jane Yolen. Little, Brown, 1998.	X	X	X	X	X	X	X	X	X	X	X	X	
The Frog Prince, Continued by Jon Scieszka. Puffin, 1991.	X	X		X		X	X	X	X	X	X	X	
The Giver by Lois Lowry. Houghton Mifflin, 1993.	X	X	X	X	X	X	X	X	X	X	X	X	X
The Magic Fan by Keith Baker. Harcourt Brace, 1989.	X	X		X	X	X	X	X	X	X	X	X	
The Three Questions by Jon J. Muth. Scholastic, 2002.	X	X	X	X		X	X	X	X	X	X	X	
There's A Hair In My Dirt! A Worm's Story by Gary Larson. Harper Perennial, 1998.	X	X		X		X	X	X	X	X		X	

Bibliography Grid (cont.)

	Cause & Effect	Character Analysis	Characteristics of . . .	Compare & Contrast	Fact, Fiction, or Opinion?	Main Idea	Mood/Feelings/Attitudes	Plot	Predictions	Sequencing	Setting	Vocabulary	Partner Books
Through the Cracks by Carolyn Sollman. Davis Pub., 1994.	X	X	X	X	X	X	X	X	X	X	X	X	
History, Freedom, and Immigration													
Amistad: A Long Road to Freedom by Walter Dean Myers. Puffin Books, 1998.	X		X	X	X		X			X	X	X	
A Picture Book of Rosa Parks by David A. Adler. Holiday House, 1993.	X	X	X	X	X	X	X			X	X	X	
Bound for America: The Forced Migration of Africans to the New World by James Haskins & Kathleen Benson. Lothrop, Lee, 1999.	X		X	X	X	X	X			X	X	X	
Building A New Land: African American in Colonial America by James Haskins and Kathleen Benson. HarperCollins, 2001.	X		X	X	X	X	X			X	X	X	
Coming to America: The Story of Immigration by Betsy C. Maestro. Scholastic, 1996.	X		X	X	X	X	X			X	X	X	
Ellis Island: Doorway to Freedom by Steven Kroll. Holiday, 1995.	X		X		X		X			X	X	X	
Escaping to America: A True Story by Rosalyn Schanzer. HarperCollins, 2000.	X	X	X	X	X	X	X	X	X	X	X	X	
Follow the Drinking Gourd by Jeanette Winter. Dragonfly, 1988.	X	X			X	X	X	X	X	X	X	X	
Freedom River by Doreen Rappaport. Hyperion Books, 2000.	X	X	X	X	X	X	X	X	X	X	X	X	
Freedom Summer by Deborah Wiles. Atheneum Books, 2001.	X	X	X	X	X	X	X	X	X	X	X	X	
From Slave Ship to Freedom Road by Julius Lester. Dial, 1998.	X			X	X		X			X	X	X	
I Have A Dream by Dr. Martin Luther King, Jr. Scholastic, 1997.	X	X	X	X	X	X	X			X		X	
Journey to Ellis Island: How My Father Came to America by Carol Bierman. Hyperion/Madison, 1998.	X	X	X	X	X	X	X	X	X	X	X	X	
Letting Swift River Go by Jane Yolen. Little Brown, 1995.	X		X	X	X	X	X	X	X	X	X	X	
Numbering All the Bones by Ann Rinaldi. Jump Sun, 2002.	X	X	X	X	X	X	X	X	X	X	X	X	X
Remembering Slavery by Ira Berlin. New Press, 2000.	X	X	X	X	X	X	X			X	X	X	
Roll of Thunder, Hear My Cry by Mildred D. Taylor. Puffin, 1976.	X	X	X	X	X	X	X	X	X	X	X	X	X
Stowaway by Karen Hesse. Scholastic Inc., 2000.	X	X	X	X	X	X	X	X	X	X	X	X	X
The Ever-Living Tree by Linda Vieira. Walker & Co., 1994.	X		X	X	X	X				X	X	X	

Bibliography Grid *(cont.)*

	Cause & Effect	Character Analysis	Characteristics of . . .	Compare & Contrast	Fact, Fiction, or Opinion?	Main Idea	Mood/Feelings/Attitudes	Plot	Predictions	Sequencing	Setting	Vocabulary	Partner Books
The Land by Mildred D. Taylor. Scholastic Inc., 2001.	X	X	X	X	X	X	X	X	X	X	X	X	X
The Pilgrims of Plimoth by Marcia Sewal. Scholastic, 1986.	X		X	X	X	X			X	X	X	X	
Through My Eyes by Ruby Bridges. Scholastic, 1999.	X	X	X	X	X	X	X	X	X	X	X	X	
We Are Americans: Voices of the Immigrant Experience by Dorothy & Thomas Hoobler. Scholastic, 2003.	X	X	X	X	X	X	X	X	X	X	X	X	
When Jessie Came Across the Sea by Amy Hest. Candlewick, 1997.	X	X	X	X	X	X	X	X	X	X	X	X	
Who Belongs Here?: An American Story by Margy Burns Knight. Tilbury House, 1993	X	X	X	X	X	X	X	X	X	X	X	X	
Legends, Myths, and Folktales													
How Turtle's Back Was Cracked by Gayle Ross. Dial Books, 1995.	X	X	X	X		X		X	X	X	X	X	
Pegasus: the Flying Horse by Jane Yolen. Dutton Books, 1998.	X	X	X	X	X	X	X	X	X	X	X	X	
Soft Child: How Rattlesnake Got Its Fangs by Joe Hayes. Harbinger House, 1993.	X	X	X	X	X	X	X	X	X	X	X	X	
The Hunter: A Chinese Folktale by Mary Casanova. Atheneum, 2000.	X	X	X	X	X	X	X	X	X	X	X	X	
The Legend of Mackinac Island by Kathy-jo Wargin. Sleeping Bear Press, 1999.	X		X	X	X	X	X	X	X	X	X	X	
The Legend of Sleeping Bear by Kathy-jo Wargin. Sleeping Bear Press, 1998.	X		X	X	X	X	X	X	X	X	X	X	
The Legend of the Loon by Kathy-jo Wargin. Sleeping Bear, 2000.	X	X	X	X	X	X	X	X	X	X	X	X	
The Story of Jumping Mouse by John Steptoe. Lothrop, Lee, 1972.	X	X	X	X	X	X	X	X	X	X	X	X	
Math													
Math Curse by Jon Scieszka. Penguin/Putnam, 1995.	X	X	X			X	X	X	X	X	X	X	
Sir Cumference and the Dragon of Pi by Cindy Neuschwander. Charlesbridge, 1999.			X			X			X	X	X		X
Sir Cumference and the First Round Table by Cindy Neuschwander. Charlesbridge, 1997.			X			X			X	X	X		X
Sir Cumference and the Great Knight of Angleland by Cindy Neuschwander. Charlesbridge, 2001.			X			X			X	X	X		X
Sir Cumference and the Sword in the Cone by Cindy Neuschwander. Charlesbridge, 2003.			X			X			X	X	X		X
The Librarian Who Measured the Earth by Kathryn Lasky. Little, Brown & Company, 1994.			X			X			X	X	X		X

Bibliography Grid (cont.)

	Cause & Effect	Character Analysis	Characteristics of . . .	Compare & Contrast	Fact, Fiction, or Opinion?	Main Idea	Mood/Feelings/Attitudes	Plot	Predictions	Sequencing	Setting	Vocabulary	Partner Books
Native Americans													
A Boy Called Slow by Joseph Bruchac. Philomel Books, 1994.	X	X	X	X	X	X	X	X	X	X	X	X	
A Picture Book of Sacagawea by David Adler. Holiday House, 2000.	X	X	X	X	X	X	X	X	X	X	X	X	
Crazy Horse's Vision by Joseph Bruchac. Lee & Low, 2000.	X	X		X	X	X				X		X	
Sacagawea by Lise Erdrich. Carolrhoda Books, 2003.	X	X	X	X	X	X	X	X	X	X	X	X	
Tecumseh by Russell Shorto. Simon & Schuster, 1989.	X	X	X	X	X	X	X	X	X	X	X	X	X
The Desert Is Theirs by Byrd Baylor. Simon & Schuster, 1975.	X		X	X	X	X				X	X	X	
The Ghost Dance by Alice McLerran. Houghton Mifflin, 1995.	X		X	X	X	X	X		X	X		X	
Walk Two Moons by Sharon Creech. HarperTrophy, 1996.	X	X	X	X	X	X	X	X	X	X	X	X	X
When Clay Sings by Byrd Baylor. Simon & Schuster, 1972.	X		X		X	X				X		X	
Poetry													
A Drop Around the World by Barbara Shaw McKinney. Dawn Publications, 1998.	X		X	X	X	X				X	X	X	
Dancers in the Garden by Joanne Ryder. Sierra Club, 1992.			X	X	X	X	X				X	X	
If I Were in Charge of the World and Other Worries by Judith Viorst. Simon & Schuster, 1981.	X		X	X		X	X					X	
Oh, the Places You'll Go! by Dr. Seuss. Random House, 1990.	X		X	X		X	X	X		X		X	
The Spider and the Fly by Tony DiTerlizzi. Scholastic, 2002.	X		X	X		X	X	X	X	X	X	X	
Way Out in the Desert by T.J. Marsh and Jennifer Ward. Northland Publishing, 1998.	X		X	X	X	X	X			X	X	X	
Welcome to the Ice House by Jane Yolen. Putnam, 2001.	X		X	X	X	X				X	X	X	
Where the Sidewalk Ends by Shel Silverstein. Harper Collins, 1974.	X		X	X		X	X			X		X	
Relationships													
A Year Down Yonder by Richard Peck. Puffin Books, 2002.	X	X	X	X	X	X	X	X	X	X	X	X	X
Amber on the Mountain by Tony Johnston. Puffin Books, 1994.	X	X	X	X	X	X	X	X	X	X	X	X	
Bridge to Terabithia by Katherine Paterson. HarperCollins, 1997.	X	X	X	X	X	X	X	X	X	X	X	X	X
Fly Away Home by Eve Bunting. Clarion Books, 1991.	X	X	X	X	X	X	X	X	X	X	X	X	
Grandfather Counts by Andrea Cheng. Lee & Low Books, 2000.	X	X				X	X	X	X	X	X	X	

Bibliography Grid *(cont.)*

	Cause & Effect	Character Analysis	Characteristics of . . .	Compare & Contrast	Fact, Fiction, or Opinion?	Main Idea	Mood/Feelings/Attitudes	Plot	Predictions	Sequencing	Setting	Vocabulary	Partner Books
Homecoming by Cynthia Voigt. Simon & Schuster, 1981.	X	X	X	X	X	X	X	X	X	X	X	X	X
My Rotten Redheaded Older Brother by Patricia Polacco. Simon & Schuster, 1994.	X	X		X	X	X	X	X	X	X	X	X	
Sadako by Eleanor Coerr. Puffin Books, 1997.	X	X	X	X	X	X	X	X	X	X	X	X	
Thundercake by Patricia Polacco. Scholastic, 1990.	X	X	X	X	X	X	X	X	X	X	X	X	
The Raft by Jim LaMarche. HarperCollins, 2000.	X	X	X	X	X	X	X	X	X	X	X	X	
The Sea Chest by Toni Buzzeo. Dial Books, 2002.	X	X		X		X	X	X	X	X	X	X	
Train to Somewhere by Eve Bunting. Scholastic, 1996.	X	X		X	X	X		X	X	X	X	X	
Where the Red Fern Grows by Wilson Rawls. Random House, 1997.	X	X	X	X	X	X	X	X	X	X	X	X	X
Science													
Bones: Our Skeletal System by Seymour Simon. Morrow, 1998.	X		X	X		X				X	X		
Cloud Dance by Thomas Locker. Harcourt Inc., 2000.	X		X	X	X	X	X				X	X	
Icebergs and Glaciers by Seymour Simon. Scholastic, 1987.	X		X	X	X					X	X	X	
Inventions That Changed the World. What a Great Idea by Stephen M. Tomecek. Scholastic, 2003.	X		X	X	X	X				X		X	
Lightning by Seymour Simon. Scholastic, 1997.	X		X	X		X			X	X	X	X	
Longitude by Dava Sobel. Penguin USA, 1996.	X	X	X	X	X	X	X	X	X	X	X	X	X
Muscles: Our Muscular System by Seymour Simon. Morrow, 1998.	X		X	X		X		X	X			X	
So You Want To Be An Inventor? by Judith St. George. Scholastic, 2002.	X		X	X		X			X	X	X	X	
Storms by Seymour Simon. Morrow, 1993.	X		X	X		X			X	X	X	X	
The Brain: Our Nervous System by Seymour Simon. Morrow, 1997.	X		X	X		X			X	X	X	X	
The Heart: Our Circulatory System by Seymour Simon. Morrow, 1996.	X		X	X		X			X	X	X		
The Perfect Storm by Sebastion Junger. Perennial, 1999.	X	X	X	X	X	X	X	X	X	X	X	X	X
Tornadoes by Seymour Simon. Scholastic, 1999.	X		X	X		X			X	X	X		
Water Dance by Thomas Locker. Harcourt, 1997.	X		X	X	X	X	X				X	X	
War													
Across Five Aprils by Irene Hunt. Berkley Publications, 1987.	X	X	X	X	X	X	X	X	X	X	X	X	X
Cecil's Story by George Ella Lyon. Orchard Books, 1991.	X	X		X	X	X	X	X	X	X	X	X	

Bibliography Grid (cont.)

	Cause & Effect	Character Analysis	Characteristics of . . .	Compare & Contrast	Fact, Fiction, or Opinion?	Main Idea	Mood/Feelings/Attitudes	Plot	Predictions	Sequencing	Setting	Vocabulary	Partner Books
Come All You Brave Soldiers by Clinton Cox. Scholastic,	X	X	X	X	X	X	X	X	X	X	X	X	X
Dear Ellen Bee: A Civil War Scrapbook of Two Union Spies by Mary E. Lyons & Muriel M. Branch. Scholastic, 2000.	X	X	X	X	X	X	X	X	X	X	X	X	X
Faithful Elephants: A True Story of Animals, People and War by Yukio Tsuchiya. Houghton Mifflin, 1997.	X	X	X	X	X	X	X	X	X	X	X	X	
Feathers and Fools by Mem Fox. Harcourt, Inc., 1989.	X	X		X	X	X	X	X	X	X	X	X	
Fields of Fury: The American Civil War by James M. McPherson. Atheneum Books, 2002.	X		X	X		X	X			X	X	X	
Hiroshima No Pika by Toshi Maruki. Morrow, 1982.	X		X	X	X	X	X	X	X	X	X	X	
My Brother Sam Is Dead by James Lincoln Collier and Christopher Collier. Four Winds, 1974.	X	X	X	X	X	X	X	X	X	X	X	X	X
Pink and Say by Patricia Polacco. Philomel Books, 1994.	X	X		X	X	X	X	X	X	X	X	X	
So Far From the Sea by Eve Bunting. Clarion Books, 1998.	X	X		X	X	X	X	X	X	X	X	X	
Soldier's Heart by Gary Paulsen. Random House, 1998.	X	X		X	X	X	X	X	X	X	X	X	
Testament: A Soldier's Story of the Civil War by Benson Bobrick. Simon & Schuster, 2003.	X	X	X	X	X	X	X	X	X	X	X	X	X
The Alamo by Shelley Tanaka. Madison Press, 2003.	X	X	X	X	X	X	X	X	X	X	X	X	X
The Bracelet by Yoshiko Uchida. Philomel Books, 1993.	X	X	X	X		X	X			X	X	X	
The Butterfly by Patricia Polacco. Philomel Books, 2000.	X	X		X	X	X	X	X	X	X	X	X	
The Wall by Eve Bunting. Clarion Books, 1990.	X	X		X	X	X	X	X	X	X	X	X	
Western Movement													
Angels in the Dust by Margot Theis Raven. Bridgewater, 2002.	X	X	X	X	X	X	X	X	X	X	X	X	
Children of the Dust Bowl: The True Story of the School at Weedpatch Camp by Jerry Stanley. Crown Publishing, 1992.	X	X	X	X	X	X	X	X	X	X	X	X	
Dandelions by Eve Bunting. Harcourt Brace, 1995.	X	X	X	X	X	X	X	X	X	X	X	X	
Out of the Dust by Karen Hesse, Scholastic, 1997.	X	X	X	X	X	X	X	X	X	X	X	X	X
Prairie Willow by Maxine Trottier. Stoddart Kids, 1998.	X	X		X	X	X	X	X	X	X	X	X	
Sunsets of the West by Tony Johnston. Putnam, 2002.	X	X		X	X	X	X	X	X	X	X	X	
The Captain's Dog: My Journey with the Lewis and Clark Tribe by Roland Smith. Harcourt, 2000.	X	X	X	X	X	X	X	X	X	X	X	X	X
The Dust Bowl by David Booth. Kids Can Press, 1997.	X	X	X	X	X	X	X	X	X	X	X	X	